GARDENING
Without Stress and Strain ✍

By JACK KRAMER

Drawings by Adrian Martinez

CHARLES SCRIBNER'S SONS
New York

Contents

Introduction: Dig It!
... But Easily ✐

In the beginning if someone would have told me I would be an avid gardener for twenty years I would have laughed at him. Yet, here I am today (after having gardens in Illinois and Florida), gardening in California and writing about it. Through the years there have been several changes in my gardening practices; I have adapted easier methods, some tricks and short-cuts which allow me to garden without undue stress or strain.

This book is about the changes I have adapted in my garden methods; the short-cuts and trial-by-experience methods I have learned to keep on my feet and off my knees and still tend a garden. Indeed, as one grows older the pleasures of a garden become more important than in former years. So no matter what your age or physical limitations, there are ways to garden, and that is what this book is all about.

I rely heavily on raised and elevated post gardens, outdoor container gardens, and in winter a fine indoor greenery. I employ natural controls such as birds and insects to keep the garden healthy so I don't have to mix, prepare, and spray dubious chemicals, and I use composts to maintain a rich soil and mulches to keep weeds away. I also believe in planning and planting the natural or informal garden which requires little work compared to the formal landscape.

Gardening without stress or strain involves more brain power than muscle power; learn how to get things done for you but always maintain absolute control. Keep your fingers in the soil but don't throw your back out of place. Exercise is important but you must realize your limitations. Dig it, but easily. Plant it, but well. And tend it always, with love.

—Jack Kramer

GARDENING
Without Stress and Strain

The author's terrace garden was planned and built so bending and stooping to tend plants is at a minimum. Paths are carefully planned so there is easy access to the terraces. (Photo by author)

1. *It's All in the Planning* ✍

Over a period of fifteen years I started three gardens of my own; each site presented different gardening problems at different ages in my life. The first garden I literally dug myself. I was young—so was my back—and the only fatality was a bee string. I planned the second garden completely on paper, but I didn't do all the digging. I had helpers. For my present garden I planned it first on paper and consulted a landscape contractor. As a result of good planning there was very little hard digging and spading but still enough physical labor to provide suitable exercise for me. Thus, this third method is the ideal one because it makes gardening easier for mind and body and saves money. It is much less trouble to follow a sketch and know where you're going than to pull up trees and shrubs or replant and do needless work.

Plan the garden slowly, and let the idea simmer a few days. Don't be afraid to seek professional help. A consultation or two with a landscape man will help you get started and then you can take it over. (And do take over since it is *your garden*!) These meetings should not be expensive—generally no more than $25 to $50 per meeting. But before you do anything, study garden catalogs because they are helpful if you know how to judge their value.

Garden Catalogs

Garden catalogs are enjoyable to read during dreary winter days. But don't just browse; make notes as you read (if you have gardened for many years you'll be doing this anyway). Some of the best catalogs on my desk and always at my elbow are those of *Wayside*

This hillside garden may seem difficult to work in; actually, the brick platform allows the gardener to tend plants easily. (Photo by Matthew Barr)

This patio-garden with built-in brick planters in graceful curving lines requires little maintenance. Plants are placed at waist level. (Photo by Ken Molino)

Gardens, Whiteflower Farm Gardens, Park Seed, and *Burpee*. (There are other good ones, but these are the ones I have worked with for years.)

When you read your catalogs, keep in mind the plant categories: perennials, annuals, bulbs, trees, and shrubs. (I'm sure you already know some of them.) It helps greatly to know plant names so you can plan your garden intelligently. If the Latin names of plants seem ponderous, keep at it; eventually you'll become acquainted with more plants than you ever thought possible. (Remember you have all winter to do it.) Knowing the correct name of a plant means you will get the plant you want.

Don't let glorious color photographs mislead you and cause visions of grandeur. It takes several years to attain the garden of your dreams, but patience is a virtue of age. That perfect garden is possible, but it takes time, planning, and work (money, too, I might add).

Do make lists of what you think you want, e.g. perennials and annuals. But remember that trees and shrubs are the most important items, so study them long and hard. They are the backbone of a garden.

Landscape Help

Few professional landscape architects will handle a small, private residential site, but a good landscape contractor, planner, or garden consultant will. No matter who you choose, ask him by phone just

The author's box garden on a deck; in planters plants are easy to weed and cultivate. More important perhaps bending is virtually eliminated. (Photo by author)

how well acquainted he is with local plant material. This is essential. You will yourself have some idea of what you want in the way of arrangement in the garden because you have pored over catalogs, studied books, and sketched.

Ask your consultant just what his fees are before he makes a visit. Ask him whether his fees include a sketch plan or merely conversation, and take it from there. Be honest and tell him you want his help to start and do not necessarily want a finished plan at the moment.

You can find these professional helpers listed in the phone book under nurseries, landscape consultants, and so forth. If that isn't successful, consult your local newspapers' classified ads. Beware of magazine ads that offer landscape assistance in the form of brochures, booklets, and schooling practices. Some of these services may be perfectly worthwhile, but I always find it wise to deal with people in my own area because they know the local flora best.

Take your time and select the man that will do the most for you (but not necessarily for the least money). You are seeking knowledge and service; make sure you get it.

Don't Do Too Much Too Fast

Once you have studied garden catalogs and books and have planned your garden on paper with or without professional help, don't rush into the garden and start digging. You want exercise, but gardening that has to be replaced is needless exercise. It is better to take the time to enjoy a vintage wine than a sprained muscle.

When the plan is finished and you are satisfied with it, decide just *who you can hire to do what best*. At this point if you say "No one can work in my garden as I do," I certainly won't dispute that. But for major construction jobs, younger people can do a better job than you. If there are beds to dig and spading to be done, of course do some, but for most muscle work *hire helpers*.

Local nurseries or classified ads list services. But again, be sure you get someone familiar with the terrain. And it is not a question of professional help but rather of getting someone willing to do hard work. Indeed, professional gardeners are scarce these days and, if located, expensive.

If you can, get some local high school students, even if it means telling them step by step what to do. Eventually they'll do it right and

Even the center planter (in foreground) allows the author to sit while gardening. Seed has been sown in the center box and has not yet germinated when this photo was taken. (Photo by author)

save you the backbreaking job of establishing the garden. There will be plenty of time to garden once things are established (or, at any rate, well under way). Seeds and perennials, bulbs and annuals are going to be with us a long time—make sure you don't hurry so you'll be around to enjoy the garden. Lay the framework first.

Once the soil is prepared to your liking (this is discussed in Chapter 3), walk your property several times to decide just where you want fences, patios, etc., it is easier to install them now rather than later. Don't let a fence throw you; there are innumerable designs available free for the asking from various wood companies.

Don't be afraid to poke around in other people's gardens to see what grows in your neighborhood. This is a grand way to avoid growing what you don't like. But don't snoop deliberately; ask first to see the garden. You'll get much information and misinformation. Just how to separate the two is a challenge, but even if you don't garner any good ideas you'll make some new friends.

If all else fails, and you can't find a local garden consultant, call the local college or botanical gardens, explain your situation, and ask some questions. People at these places are always more than willing to help. Don't ask them to plan your garden; keep your questions simple: which plants will or will not grow in your area.

2. Tools and Special Aids 🌿

I think we all—young and old—pretty much realize that having the proper tools and aids (and all in *one* place) for a job is half the battle of gardening. It saves wear and tear on the muscles and needless swearing—you can conserve your energy for the actual gardening job. But there are so many different kinds of hand tools—hoes and rakes, spades and shovels—that selecting the right type almost becomes a paramount problem. And the right decision *is* necessary; when a long-handled shovel splits in two in a youngster's hand there is little physical damage, but in less agile hands it could mean broken bones.

There is also an endless selection of power tools. In fact, there are so many, from electric hedge clippers to lawn vacuum machines, that garden magazines devote pages to them yearly. However, you can skip these pages since you need only a few important power tools (which we shall discuss in a later section).

Greenhouses are of course not an essential part of gardening, but they are a great convenience in many ways: In them you can start plants, sow seed, start cuttings, harden plants, and so forth, without ever bending! That alone makes a small greenhouse essential for me. (See Chapter 10 for a more detailed discussion of these useful structures.) Finally, there are also garden helpers that you yourself can make and special aids that make gardening more enjoyable.

HOES, RAKES, AND OTHER HAND TOOLS

There are many kinds of hoes; a few are indispensable because of their usefulness. For example, a hoe takes the bending out of weed-

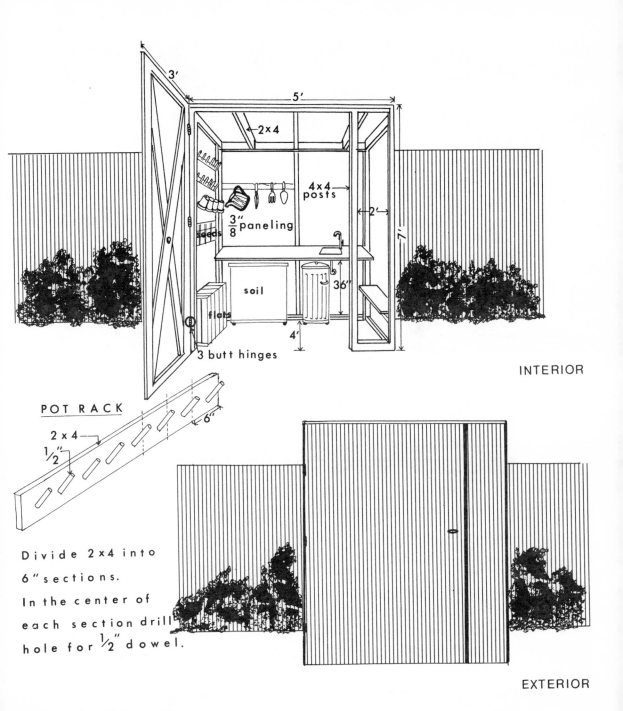

3'

5'

2 x 4

4 x 4 posts

2'

7'

$\frac{3}{8}$" paneling

seeds

36"

soil

flats

4'

3 butt hinges

INTERIOR

POT RACK

2 x 4

$\frac{1}{2}$"

6"

Divide 2 x 4 into
6" sections.
In the center of
each section drill
hole for $\frac{1}{2}$" dowel.

EXTERIOR

Plant Shed

Spading soil is good exercise but don't overdo it; select tools that feel comfortable in your hands. (Photo courtesy O. M. Scott Co.)

ing, and although you can't get out all the weeds with a hoe, you can, after some experience, get most of them. Hoes are also good for breaking up dry soils and making furrows. You really don't need the standard, wide-bladed, and scuffle hoes, but definitely get a weeding hoe and a Warren hoe because they are great labor savers. What brand you buy depends on what is available in your local area, but do buy the best you can afford. And remember to *hold* the hoe first; the weights of hoes vary and the length of the handle should suit your body stature.

Rakes are more important than most people think. By the way, raking the garden of debris and lawn clippings and smoothing the soil is fine exercise for almost everyone. I have several—leaf, iron-pronged, grass, self-cleaning, pronged, and spading rakes (and no doubt a few more I have forgotten)—because they have innumerable uses. I use a level-headed iron rake for breaking up soil and a springy bow rake for cleaning debris. Avoid bamboo rakes since they are troublesome and invariably break after a few months of use. I find the iron-pronged rake is good for breaking up hard soil and for light weeding and cultivating jobs. Once again, buy the best you can afford, and look for good balance and heavy-duty materials.

Although you might think you won't be using spades and shovels, there will be times when even your most trusted garden boy just doesn't do what you want him to—*you* will be pressed into service. The most useful shovels include the round headed and square bladed; the helpful spades are the trench, regular, narrow, and small. When making your selection, keep in mind that shovels and spades are designed for scooping, digging, lifting, and mixing soils. I use only a round-pointed shovel for digging and a square or regular spade

A heavy duty tool that can be used for raking, digging, cleaning. (Photo courtesy Scott Laen Products)

for adding soil amendments, turning soil, and sometimes even for weeding. The handles of shovels and spades are long, short, or shaped like a "D"; use the shape that is most comfortable.

Generally hand trowels are pointed, rounded, or flat edged, scoop or spatula shaped. Buy a *sturdy* trowel since working hard soil will bend shanks on all but the best, and select a well-balanced trowel that fits your hand.

Pruning tools too come in a variety of models; there are border, grass, pruning and lopping shears, to mention some. There are also

Select tools for their uses; this spading fork is fine for cultivating soil. (Photo courtesy O. M. Scott Co.)

hedge shears (four different kinds), pruning saws (four different kinds), and pole saws (two different kinds). Confusing, isn't it? Well, let's simplify it. In twenty years of gardening although I have purchased many pruning tools, I only use three kinds. I have a small pruning shears; this is the basic pruning tool for countless light cutting jobs. I also use a lopping shears more than I thought I would; these have a long handle and give you more cutting strength than a one-hand shears. I use this tool to cut small limbs, branches, etc. My third tool is a pruning saw to cut small limbs and branches.

Pole pruners and pole saws for sawing branches high overhead should be avoided. Cutting trees with these long-handled gadgets is not wise. There is just too much chance of accidents. Hedge and border shears I suppose are necessary to some people but I have never had occasion to use them. I manage fine with my small pruning shears.

Note that all tools should be kept clean and free of rust—after using tools always wipe away soil and dry any metal parts. Occasionally oil tools to keep them in tip-top shape.

Power Tools

This section is purposely short because power tools, although designed for convenience and labor saving, are difficult to operate and store, and costly. As mentioned, a few power tools are vital to the gardener, but most aren't. Forget cleaning machines, garden tillers, tractors, chain saws, and elaborate electric mowers. Probably all you really need is a cordless electric hedge-and-shrub trimmer and maybe a lightweight electric garden vacuum, which saves much labor. So don't let glitter and gleam tempt you; use your good judgment and buy only what you need.

My Garden Helper

It has been said that a little bending never hurt anyone. This is *generally* true, but for people with back trouble bending is a difficult task. A few years ago I visited several lumber companies—I wanted something that would relieve the strain on my back muscles and hold tools and me when my hands had to be near the soil for weeding and planting. (I had tried a wooden stool, but invariably I had to run back and forth for tools.) The solution was a low bench (twelve

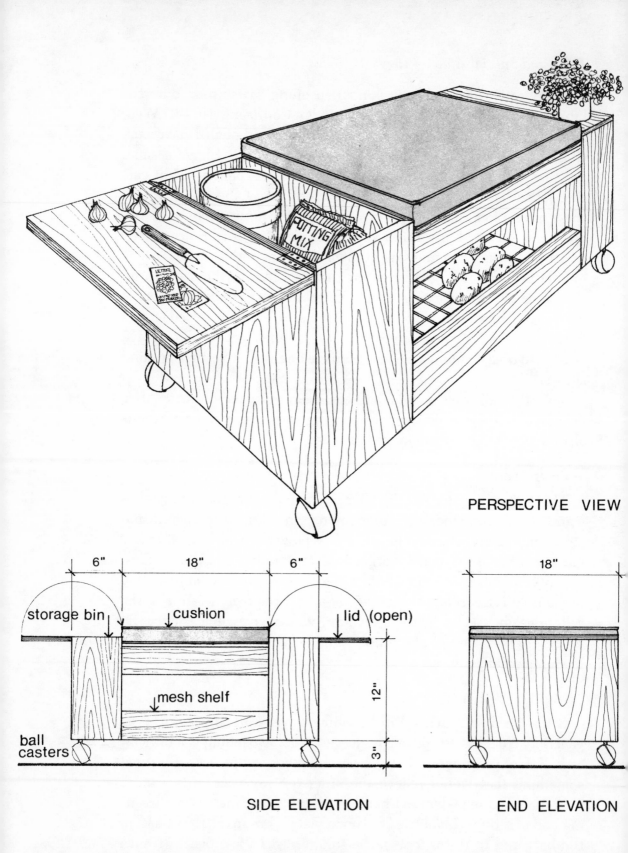

PERSPECTIVE VIEW

6"   18"   6"

storage bin   cushion   lid (open)

mesh shelf   12"

ball casters   3"

SIDE ELEVATION

18"

END ELEVATION

Portable Garden Stool

DESIGN: ADRIÁN MARTÍNEZ

A garden vacuum takes the labor out of cleaning the yard; while not essential, it is helpful. (Photo courtesy Gilson Co.)

inches high and eighteen inches across) that I built that enabled me to be next to the ground I was working when I was seated. I put my tools in storage bins in the sides of the stool. This portable bench was equipped with ball casters so it could be moved easily without lifting it. (A drawing of the bench is on page 16.)

SPECIAL AIDS

A good pair of gloves is a must because you will be handling soil, rocks, weeds, and sometimes thorny plants. Cloth and plastic gloves are useful, but unfortunately they usually come in only two sizes:

large or small, so get leather gloves—they are available in several sizes. Make sure the gloves don't slip from the hands and that they aren't too tight.

I used to scoff at the idea of knee pads, but I don't any more because when I must kneel I find that the foam-rubber knee pads (sold at nurseries) are quite comfortable and save the knees from stone bruises and unnecessary pavement attacks. Shop before you buy though, and pick the pads that tie securely in place; some knee pads are impossible to tie and end up on your ankles, which is hardly good for gardening!

Try to obtain a carpenter's apron for wear in the garden. This handy piece of clothing has pockets and loops for tools. It has saved me much walking; I can carry shears, fertilizer packets, and an assortment of things I always seem to need while gardening. Some lumber stores sell carpenter's aprons, but most don't. Nevertheless, keep searching—they are well worth the effort.

A wheelbarrow should not be a special aid; it is really a necessity in a garden and I use it for numerous things. I haul soil in it, move plants in it, mix cement in it, and generally use it whenever I want to carry things and not lift them. By all means buy the best wheelbarrow you can afford. There are three or four models in several

This miner's pick has a dozen uses in the garden: weeding, cultivating, digging planting holes and so forth. Heavy duty leather gloves are also essential when working in the garden. (Photo by Matthew Barr)

price brackets. Two of the less expensive wheelbarrows lasted exactly three months before the wheel gave way and was unrepairable. My expensive wheelbarrow ($59.50) has served me for eight years now.

In closing this chapter let me mention a miner's or camper's pick a friend suggested to me for gardening. This simple tool can be used for a multitude of garden chores: digging, spading, weeding, chopping, and cultivating. It should be called the gardener's friend but unfortunately is not available at garden stores. You'll find it in surplus stores that carry camping and hiking gear. Get one and try it. I think you'll agree with me that it is an indispensable garden aid.

3. *Plant Growth, Climate, and Soil* ✑

Get acquainted with plants—know how they grow and what makes them grow—so you can care for them intelligently. It saves much unneccessary labor. A little knowledge about roots, stems, and leaves, and how they work together takes the mystery out of plants.

This chapter is not a technical treatise of plant growth. It explains in simple terms just what makes a plant grow and how it assimilates its food. If you know what does what in a plant you can become your own plant doctor and can avoid panic if plants don't grow as they should. You will have some idea what is wrong with an ailing plant and how to take care of it.

Another part of successful gardening is knowing your climate. Knowledge of weather in your area can save you work and energy since climate dictates what you can and can't grow. Remember, working with nature makes gardening a pleasure; working against her is a chore.

Basic Principles of Plant Growth

Plants live on a liquid diet, so any nutrients they get must be in liquid form, and the liquid must get to the roots. The roots absorb water and chemical substances that are necessary for plant growth; if roots don't get water the plant dies.

The roots work in partnership with the leaves. The leaf factory combines gas and liquid. In one form or another the leaves obtain oxygen, hydrogen, carbon, nitrogen, and other elements. (Water supplies the hydrogen and oxygen; carbon comes from the roots as humus in the soil.)

20

The leaves make organic food out of sunlight, air, water, and earth salts—this manufacturing process is called photosynthesis: the energy of the sun is changed into a form that can be used in the life process of the plant. Chlorophyll (the green matter in plants) is the catalyst; it transforms carbon dioxide, water, and the energy of the sun and produces sugars and carbohydrates. (Leaf activity also includes transpiration of the loss of water as vapor.)

The stem and trunks store, distribute, and process the products of the leaves and roots of nearly all plants. Before this storing process takes place the sugar must be transformed into starch or other complicated proteins, oils, and waxes.

BUYING PLANTS

It pays to buy the very best possible plants because they are more liable to succeed. Hundreds of plants are available at nurseries and from mail-order suppliers. Seedling annuals and perennials are sold in flats or cartons (these are shallow wood or plastic containers). Your best buy is a flat of fifty or sixty plants. If you don't want to start your own plants from seed (which takes additional work and effort), seedlings in flats are a blessing. I sit on the small bench I made with the flat resting on an angled plywood board in my lap so I am at the height of the soil and can do my planting without backbreaking effort.

Shrubs and trees are sold balled and burlapped (B&B) or bare root. With the B&B method, a tree is dug from the ground with a ball of soil around it; it is then wrapped in burlap and tied at the crown with a string. Evergreen shrubs, conifers, and some deciduous shrubs are sold this way (see Chapter 7 for more information).

Plants sold in cans are at nurseries during all the seasons and come in a variety of sizes and prices. Remember to have the cans cut at the nursery and to get the plant in the ground right away. You can't extricate the plant from its container without a can cutter; if you try you'll ruin the plant and your disposition.

Generally, nurseries will load your car for you, but since unloading at home is your job don't buy anything that will be too heavy to carry. Flats and cartons of seedlings fit easily in your car trunk or back seat (have the nurseryman protect your car from soil with paper liners). Don't lift large trees and shrubs; ideally you should have them delivered, but if you insist on carrying large plants in your car, make sure they don't obstruct your view.

Don't leave the newly purchased plants sitting in the garden in sun; it weakens some and kills others (only a few don't mind). The shock of transplanting is enough for the plant to contend with in the beginning, so don't burden it unnecessarily. If plants are being delivered, make sure you or someone is there to receive them so they can be planted right away.

CLIMATE AND PLANTS

The advent of new gardening aids—fertilizers, insecticides, and other chemicals—has caused many people to lose sight of what gardening really is. Too often the homeowner sprinkles, sprays, feeds, and protects his plants in an endless program. But none of the new products are miracle workers; gardening is still working with nature, which includes climate.

Your area's climate has a tremendous influence on what kind of plants you can grow. Know how much rainfall your locale receives. (One of the blessings of arthritis is that you can forecast your climate by how stiff your bones feel!) Sun, humidity, wind, and seasonal characteristics too are all part of the gardening program. In every region, climatic factors are different—even in a ten-mile radius climate can vary considerably, especially if you are near hills, lakes, and streams. For example, my house is only fourteen miles from San Francisco. In summer the temperature is fifteen degrees warmer here than it is in the city. Our annual rainfall is about thirty-eight inches; in the city it is about seventeen inches.

The East Coast has similar climatic differences within its own regions because of its varied topography. In the South, where moderate temperatures prevail all year, there is still another kind of gardening picture. Thus, a wise gardener, unlike the neophyte, will write for specific maps (available from the Weather Bureau) of his state.

Climate can be modified somewhat of course. You cannot stop the wind, but you can stop its harmful effects. Stop branch breaking by having trees properly pruned. Grow fruit trees (which can be harmed by wind) in espalier fashion against walls and fences, and have hedges put in place to break the force of the wind.

If you are in a rainy area, be sure that sufficient drainage has been provided. The soil will be constantly leached, so be prepared to add fertilizer often. And in dry regions with scanty rainfall, remember that plants to some degree adapt to water shortage.

If there is too much sun, plant under trees or to the north of the building, but expect a reduction of flowering in plants. Provide a means of combating loss of moisture, which is the chief effect of excess sun (mulching the soil helps a great deal).

SOIL AND SOIL TESTING

Soil is the basis of practically all gardening. Although Japanese gardens may have only rocks and sand, most gardens have plants, trees, and shrubs. However, you can start to landscape only when the soil is properly prepared.

Earth or soil has two layers: topsoil and subsoil. The subsoil is beneath the surface layer; it has been there for hundreds of years, and it can be either a few inches or as much as twenty inches below the surface. The subsoil varies greatly in composition: it is sandy or claylike. A very sandy subsoil that retains little moisture is useless to plants. If it is very clayey, the subsoil holds water so long that plants literally drown. It should be broken up, or for severe cases a drainage system should be installed.

A fertile topsoil, which is a mixture of clay, sand, and humus, is porous in texture and provides good drainage. Because it is spongy

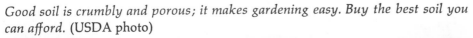

Good soil is crumbly and porous; it makes gardening easy. Buy the best soil you can afford. (USDA photo)

the soil retains moisture; the humus provides good conditions for the growth of soil bacteria, which is essential for plant nutrition. This is the kind of soil we want in our garden, but in most cases it must be built by a program of soil conditioning.

A good soil has excellent water absorption, thus enabling moisture to be transported quickly through the pores to the roots of the plant where it is stored for future use. The pores also carry away excess water, thus preventing the topsoil from becoming soggy. Once soil is waterlogged, air can't circulate freely, and circulation is necessary for good plant growth.

Good drainage is essential for preventing a waterlogged situation that can kill plants because they develop shallow roots and perish from a lack of moisture since they can't reach down for the stored water. Poor drainage is a common fault of most soils and is generally caused by a layer of hard earth.

Improve the physical structure of the soil by turning it, keeping it porous, and using composts and mulches throughout the year. Porosity is the key to good soil; only when little air tubes are in the soil is it worthwhile to fertilize and work your garden. Fertility alone won't provide for good plant growth; the physical condition or tilth of the soil is just as important in the overall working of the soil.

Dig up some soil on your property and crumble it in your hand. If it is lumpy and claylike you must add sand and humus. If it is sandy and falls apart in your hand you have to add some organic matter. A good soil crumbles between the fingers and feels like a well-done baked potato: porous with good texture.

Humus

Humus—animal manure, compost, leaf mold, and peat moss—is living organisms or their decayed remains. Humus adds body to light soils and provides aeration for clayey soils. It dissolves in the soil and provides nourishment for plants and microorganisms. It is constantly used and depleted and must be replaced, so maintenance of the proper proportion of humus in the soil is vital to good plant growth.

A convenient source of humus is peat moss, which is available at nurseries. There are differences between the various types of peat available, but through the years I have used many kinds and they

Always spade and till soil (or have someone do it) so it has good tilth. It is vital to health of plants. (USDA photo)

all proved satisfactory. Leaf mold, another source of humus, is decayed leaves and grass clippings. Rake leaves into a pile and let them decompose. A third excellent source of humus is compost, which is basically decayed vegetable matter. (Composts are fully discussed in the next Chapter.)

You must be your own judge about how much humus to add to soil. The amount depends on the soil, the kind of plants being grown, and the existing content of the humus. I mix about one inch of compost to about six inches of soil; this has proven satisfactory through the years for my garden.

Even though you add humus to the soil, you also have to use

Here, humus has been added to soil; note how dark the soil is, rich and crumbly. (Photo by author)

fertilizers as a supplement. Fertilizers contain nitrogen, phosphorus, and potassium (potash). But fertilizers are not substitutes for humus, nor can decayed organic matter completely do the work of fertilizers —soil needs both.

pH Scale

The pH scale is like a thermometer, but instead of measuring heat it measures the acidity or alkinity of soil. Soil with a pH of 7 is neutral; below 7 the soil is acid, and above 7 it is alkaline.

It is important to know what kind of soil you have so that the maximum results of all fertilizers supplied to it can be obtained. To determine the pH of your garden soil, have it tested by the state agricultural authorities or make your own test with one of the kits available from suppliers.

Most of our commonly grown trees and shrubs prefer a neutral soil; some grow better in an acid condition, and several types prefer an alkaline soil. But generally a soil reaction as nearly neutral as possible (between 6 and 7) allows you to grow the most plants successfully.

In alkaline soils potash becomes less and less effective and eventually becomes locked in. In very acid soils aluminum becomes so active that it becomes toxic to plants. Acidity in soil controls many functions: (1) it governs the availability of the food in the soil and determines which bacteria thrive in it, and (2) it somewhat affects the rate at which roots can take up moisture and leaves can manufacture food.

To lower the pH of soil (increase the acidity), apply ground sulfur at the rate of 1 pound to 100 square feet. (This lowers the pH symbol of loam soil about one point.) Spread the sulfur on top of the soil and then apply water.

To raise (sweeten) the pH of soil, add ground limestone at the rate of 10 pounds per 150 square feet. Scatter the limestone on the soil, or mix it well with the top few inches of soil and water. It is better to add ground limestone or hydrated lime in several applications at six- or eight-week intervals instead of using a lot at one time.

Soil testing kits are available from suppliers or at nurseries. (Photo courtesy Sudbury Lab.)

Here, lime is being spread to condition soil. A necessary step (and easily done) to sweeten soil and lessen acidity. (USDA photo)

WATERING

Water is the lifeline of a plant, and it must reach plant roots in sufficient quantity. Don't think you can keep your garden growing by hand sprinkling a few minutes a day—it won't work.

Even though completely automatic watering devices are wonderful, few people can afford them, so generally you must rely on sprinklers. But be careful—I have a friend who is constantly running back and forth adjusting sprinklers and invariably getting drenched. He ends the day totally exhausted! This is not the way to water plants unless you are racing toward a heart attack.

Because there are so many kinds of sprinklers, do some investigation before you buy one. You want one that will save you work and time. Once placed, it should stay there so that all you have to do is go out once and turn on the faucets.

I took a lesson from the highway planting department and invested in what is known as a Rain Bird. This unit throws water at great velocity in a circular pattern. It will take a few trial runs before you find the right place for the Rain Bird, that is, a place where it is "raining" on the right amount of the property, but once in place the "bird" can be left and turned on with a flick of the hand.

Another type of watering device is the oscillating sprinkler, which throws water in alternating waves from side to side; this provides soil with a thorough soaking without forming puddles on the ground. These devils, though, are rather difficult to set because they have a hand-operated control that reads "left," "right," or "center," only approximating where the water is to fall. But like the Rain Bird, the oscillating sprinkler can be left in place.

Depending on the size of your property you will need one, two, or more sprinklers. I have almost a half acre of three gardens and I use four sprinklers: two oscillating types and two Rain Birds, which seems to work fine.

Hoses (used to deliver water to sprinklers) are another vital part of gardening, although they may not seem so until you start to move them around. Today, thanks to American ingenuity, there are many kinds of hoses, but basically the old-fashioned types are still the only good ones. The plastic hose, unless handled with great care, and the flat hose invariably wiggle around. Buy a good, sturdy-type rubber hose. It will last and last, is easily handled, can be mistreated and pushed around without undue damage.

4. How to Avoid Unnecessary Work ✍

Working in the garden is good exercise for both the body and the mind. However, experience and time will teach you how to avoid doing unnecessary things so that your time can be utilized doing other more-interesting gardening (and in the end the garden and you profit). For example, use mulches to protect plants and cut down on weeding, add good compost to your soil to avoid unnecessary spading and digging of old earth, and follow the proven ways of moving and handling large tubs and boxes.

MULCHES

A mulch is a covering of organic or inorganic material laid on exposed soil (generally around plants) in your garden. Grass clippings, leaf mold, shells, hulls of rice, peanut hulls, sawdust, or hay and straw are all organic mulches; that is, they decay in time and return to the soil. Inorganic mulches include newspapers, aluminum foil, and plastic sheeting.

Mulching does many things. It conserves moisture and also keeps the soil temperature cool in summer and warm in winter. Mulching discourages weeds and prevents a hard top crust from forming on soil. A mulch also protects plants from alternating freezing and thawing in winter, which can harm plants. And, above all, an organic mulch eventually decays and adds nutrients to your soil.

TYPES

There are many kinds of mulches, but the following seven are the most popular:

1. *Hay and straw*   These are inexpensive, deteriorate slowly, are lightweight, and easy to apply. (Salt hay is weed free, too.)

2. *Leaves*   Leaves make a good mulch, but remember to occasionally poke holes in the covering so air reaches the leaves or they can form a soggy wet covering. Oak leaves and pine needles are excellent for acid-loving plants such as rhododendrons and azaleas.

3. *Peat*   This widely used but expensive mulch smothers weeds effectively and holds water, but it can become an impervious mat that hinders water from reaching the soil.

4. *Cocoa beans and peanut shells*   Both these materials, when decomposed, add important nitrogen, phosphorus, and potash to the soil. They are easy to scatter, are not objectionable to look at, and are generally inexpensive.

5. *Tree bark*   This comes in many grades, but the medium-sized pellets are best. The bark decomposes slowly, is neat, and looks good

Mulches for plants may be hay or straw, cocoa bean shells, etc. Here wood chips are used. These are organic and in time will return to the soil. (USDA photo)

in the garden. Once it was inexpensive but lately has increased tremendously in price.

6. *Sawdust*   Use it by itself or add it to other mulches.

7. *Inorganic mulches*   These do not add anything to the soil, but where they are available they can be used. Inorganic mulches include:

(*a*) *Stones and pebbles*   Water passes through stones and pebbles, and plant roots are protected from temperature changes. They have the added bonus of being decorative.

(*b*) *Polyethylene film*   This material—black or white—is difficult to set in place and eventually curls, so it is hardly attractive. If you use it, be sure to punch some holes in it so water can penetrate to the soil; otherwise it may do more harm than good. Cover it with small pebbles or fir bark to keep it anchored to the ground.

(*c*) *Newspapers*   Laid flat in place on the ground, newspapers make

Plants are being mulched with straw in this photo. (USDA photo)

a better mulch than you may think. They may not look attractive, but they do the job.

(*d*) *Aluminum foil*   In my opinion this is much too expensive to use for mulching.

Mulches can be used advantageously on all plants except grasses and ground covers. Do not cover the crowns of the plants when spreading mulches; pile the material two to three inches thick up to the base of the plant. In California, we keep mulches in place all year, and I suggest this procedure for most parts of the country. However, if you can't keep the mulches in place all year, apply them after the soil has warmed up in spring and after growth has started. If put on too early they may hinder growth somewhat because they tend to keep the soil cool. In fall, apply mulches after the soil has frozen.

Composts

A compost pile in most gardens seems undesirable, which is perhaps why they are seldom seen and why many gardeners have problems with soil and plants. Yet composting is a basic of successful gardening. Composting is making your own fertilizer and soil conditioner by using garden wastes such as twigs and leaves and kitchen wastes and whatever other organic material you don't want. The compost pile not only saves you money (you don't have to buy humus), but it saves time and labor. A garden with composted soil is always a healthy garden, so you can avoid the chores of combating insects and tending unhealthy plants.

If you are squeamish about having the compost pile as part of the garden (because of odors), hide it near the garden but close enough so you can get to it. A small 5 x 5-feet bin can be constructed somewhere on the property to confine the compost or you can buy commercial metal compost units.

To build your own bins for composting, use 2 x 12-inch planks set inside 4 x 4-inch posts and fixed on three sides. Leave the fourth side open or have a gate in it for easy access. Concrete blocks may also be used to fashion a bin.

To start the compost add garden debris: raked leaves, twigs, and branches. Over this sprinkle some soil and then some manure. (Manure now comes in tidy packages at nurseries for the fastidious.)

A compost pile is made by piling vegetable and other garden refuse in layers with soil, an excellent way to have rich compost to add to soil. (USDA photo)

Build up layers, and sprinkle some lime on each layer. Air is needed within the compost heap to keep organisms working, so from time to time punch holes into the heap with a broom handle. Be sure moisture gets to the heap too, but never saturate it. If you don't have enough rain, occasionally sprinkle the heap with water. After a few months, turn the heap, bringing the sides to the top. When you apply compost put it on top of the soil and hoe it slightly; the idea is to leave the organic matter near the surface. Don't bury it.

A more-sophisticated method of making a compost heap involves putting materials through a shredder (available at garden suppliers); this speeds up the process considerably. You might want to also try chemicals that hasten the decaying process. They are available at nurseries under different trade names.

MOVING CONTAINERS

Recently, while moving, I had a large rhododendron (almost eight feet tall) in a twenty-eight-inch tub. Since it was a favorite plant I wanted to take it with me, but it weighed at least six hundred pounds. To further add to my consternation, the plant was on a hillside about twelve feet from the ground. Even two strong backs (hired help) wouldn't be able to do the job. But an old Chinese gardener working across the street suggested the solution. He looked at the plant and muttered "Slide it down on planks." I nodded and went about my business, but the next day I realized the validity of his idea. I had two

The author's compost pile at the edge of the property; a bin to contain and hide the compost is generally the best procedure if neighbors are nearby. (Photo by author)

1. tip planter & bunch sack under

2. tip opposite way & pull out sack

3. proceed to drag planter

DRAG W/ BURLAP SACK

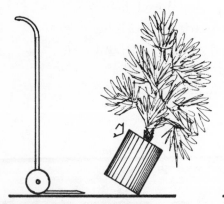

1. tip planter & slide in truck

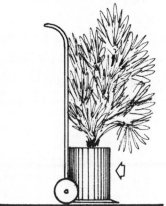

2. seat snugly against back

3. tip truck back and push

PUSH W/ HAND TRUCK

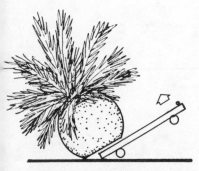

1. tip planter & slide dolly under

2. push planter to centre

3. pull dolly w/ rope

PULL W/ DOLLY

Moving Container Plants

boys who were working in my yard get two 2 x 12-inch redwood boards twelve feet long and prop them at the base of the container. The trick was to lift the box only once, just two or three inches, to get it on the boards. They did this in a few minutes, and I guided the planter and plant as it slid down the boards and rested in the yard. We were halfway home now.

The next step was to get the planter on a truck. I remember the old burlap-bag method: pulling the plant. I put the bag on the pavement next to the plant. Once more the boys lifted the planter an inch or so onto the burlap; the rest was easy. We pulled the box across the yard to the truck. To get it on the truck we again propped the 2 x 12-inch boards against the truck floor and pushed the plant on the truck.

Now when one of my fellow gardeners says I can't possibly move containers I say "Think again." Most containers can be moved to another place on burlap and pulled across an area. Or ease boxes and tubs along on two-inch steel poles. This is a slow procedure, but it works and saves back and leg work. Set two rollers under the box, and start pushing the container along. Replace rollers as you continue the move. By the way, wooden dollies and casters for containers won't work in the garden unless you have pavement under them.

PERSPECTIVE VIEW

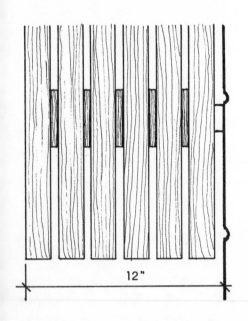

12"

END DETAIL

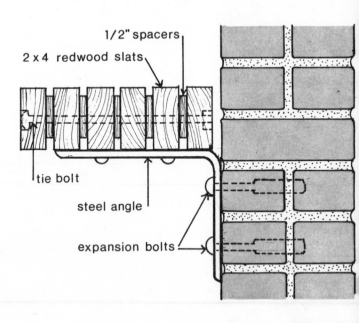

1/2" spacers

2 x 4 redwood slats

tie bolt

steel angle

expansion bolts

SECTION

Shelf Garden

DESIGN : ADRIÁN MARTÍNEZ

5. No-Bend Gardening: Raised Planters ✐

Raised planters (at waist level or higher) let you easily tend plants; for our school of gardeners this is reward enough—no more backaches and tedious bending! But there are other reasons for the popularity of elevated gardens: they allow for versatility when planning the garden; they relieve the monotony of a ground garden; and they put flowers and plants in a position that delights the eye.

Included in this chapter about raised planters are discussions about window boxes, step gardens, and shelf gardens. Thus you'll discover old ways and new ways to enjoy your yard without straining the muscles. Raised planters give you the opportunity to work your garden and get enough but not too much exercise to cause concern.

Making planters may seem complicated and beyond your prowess, but simple planters can be built easily in an afternoon. Or, of course, you can have them made by a handyman or a carpenter.

Outdoor Planters and Beds

Because the planter or raised bed becomes part of the design of the garden it should be planned carefully, with scale and balance kept in mind. Again, sketches on paper will help to decide just how to arrange and how many planters are necessary. A simple design is best because it can be used with almost any style of architecture while providing a good home for plants. We mention several kinds of planters in this chapter, but remember that you will have to design planters to your own specification, which will vary depending on the site. A planter may be a window box or a raised unit that runs the entire length of the house, an arrangement of modular boxes, a step garden, and so forth. What you choose depends on the house and the site. In any case, the material for the planter should be impervious to the weather. Redwood or cypress is generally used because these materials do not need preservatives and yet weather beautifully and last for years. Stone and concrete are other good materials.

Outdoor planters can be freestanding or of a stationary type of any given design—triangular, oblong, or rectangular. Freestanding boxes are instant gardening when used for patio borders or in corners; with geraniums and agapanthus, the patio becomes colorful in one afternoon. And portable units can be rearranged at any time—put them where you think they will look best.

Brick, stone, or slate stationary planters take time to make, but once built they are attractive, especially against a house wall. A trench about twenty inches in depth must be dug, depending on the local frost line of the area.

Wooden Planters

Wood is a favorite material for raised planters and beds; it is easy to work with, generally inexpensive in most areas, is easily handled, hardly breaks or chips, blends well in the garden, and, as mentioned, redwood and cypress tolerate weather and improve in appearance with age.

Because plant boxes come in many shapes, specific areas can be accommodated with boxes. The planters may be portable or can be affixed to become part of the garden design. Boxes can be stacked in tiers, arranged in grid fashion against the wall for easy gardening that eliminates stooping and squatting, or combined with longer or deeper ones to provide dimension and attractiveness, especially in small spaces. In fact, boxes are so versatile that there is no end to their uses for gardeners.

The thickness of the lumber you use depends on the box to be built; smaller boxes to 16 x 24-inches can be made with one-inch lumber. Larger boxes are best when made with two-inch lumber. Use galvanized nails or brass screws when building planters. In the following pages we show many box-construction designs that you can apply to your garden.

Another variation of a plant box is the L-shaped container; combine wood and concrete to provide a gardening area against a house or garage corner. The back walls of these containers should be of brick or concrete to help ward off termites, and all wood should be kept at least six inches above soil line. You can also make divided and multilevel L-shaped containers, and there are dozens of ways to vary the arrangement to make it pleasing to the eye.

Terraced containers aren't difficult to make. They add great dimension to the garden, and if cleverly planned, with steps adjoining or dividing them, they are a blessing. Railroad ties are frequently used for this type of construction; the results are infinitely charming.

No matter how you decide to use plant boxes in your garden, you will find they take the ache out of gardening and contribute a great deal to an area. And don't think you can't make them yourself.

These boxes are simple to make; redwood is the material; some lumber companies will precut lumber to size so only nailing and screws have to be inserted. (Photo by author)

Another photo of home-made planter boxes; note platform on bottoms to allow air to enter bottom of boxes and to eliminate hiding places of insects. (Photo by author)

Small boxes are well within the realm of our kind of gardening, but larger boxes—and these are useful too—can be made by a handyman or a carpenter. The initial cost may be high, but remember that these boxes will be with you for many years.

Masonry Boxes

Planters can also be made of various masonry materials like brick, fieldstone, flagstone, concrete blocks, and so forth. Masonry is solid, heavy, always durable, and may be held together by cement or be of dry-wall construction (without mortar). Basically, masonry planters are either built-up in layers with brick or concrete block and mortar or by pouring wet cement into wooden forms.

Install all these structures on a concrete footing that has been poured into a trench dug in the ground. This footing carries the weight of the wall and prevents it from turning over. In cold climates, where soil freezes, the footing *must* go below the frost line.

If you decide to tackle building a masonry planter, have the necessary trenches dug because this is hard and possibly exhausting work. To build the planter, lay out a string line of the shape you want and then have a trench dug six to twenty inches deep on this line (and

PERSPECTIVE VIEW

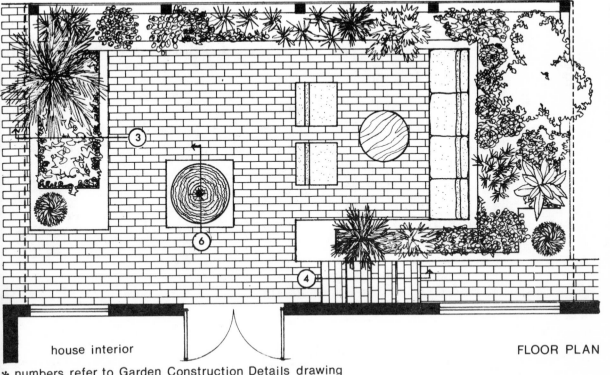

house interior

FLOOR PLAN

*numbers refer to Garden Construction Details drawing

Lath Garden Room

DESIGN: ADRIÁN MARTÍNEZ

PERSPECTIVE VIEW

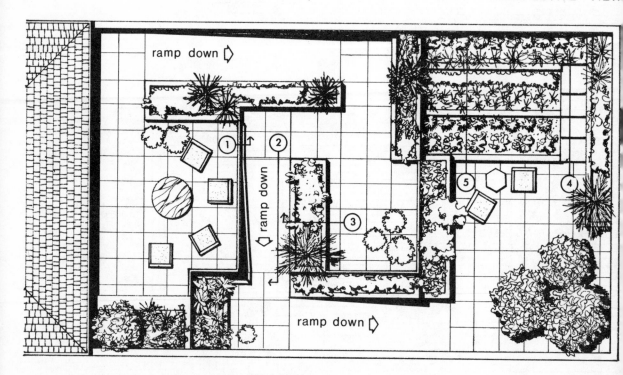

ramp down ▷

① ↑
②

ramp down ◁

③

⑤ ④

ramp down ▷

∗ numbers refer to Garden Construction Details drawing

SITE PLAN

Garden w/Ramps & Terraces

DESIGN: ADRIÁN MARTÍNEZ

PERSPECTIVE VIEW

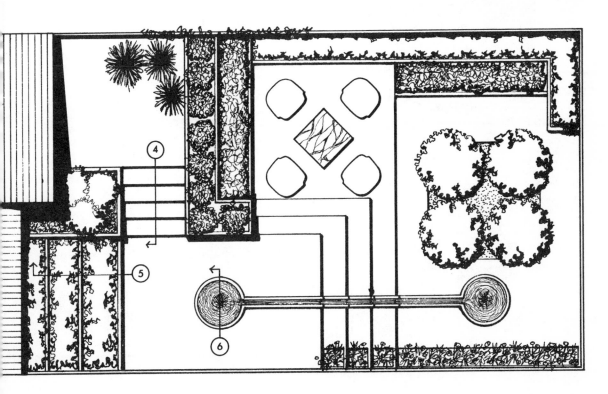

numbers refer to Garden Construction Details drawing

SITE PLAN

Stepped Garden

DESIGN: ADRIÁN MARTÍNEZ

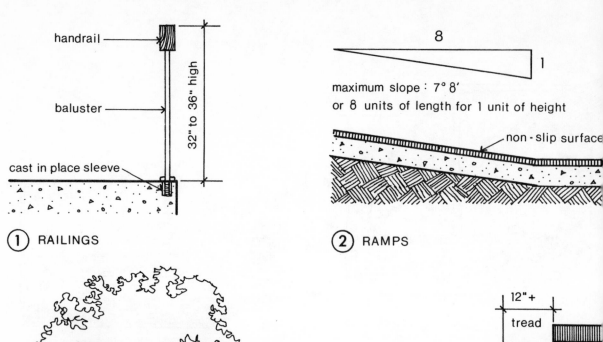

handrail

baluster

32" to 36" high

cast in place sleeve

①　RAILINGS

8

1

maximum slope : 7° 8′
or 8 units of length for 1 unit of height

non‑slip surface

②　RAMPS

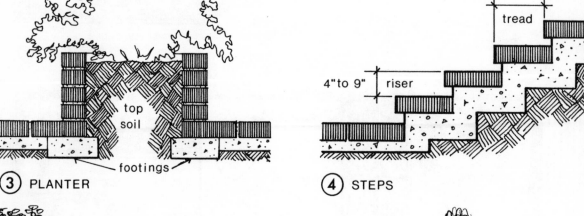

top
soil

footings

③　PLANTER

12"+

tread

4"to 9"　riser

④　STEPS

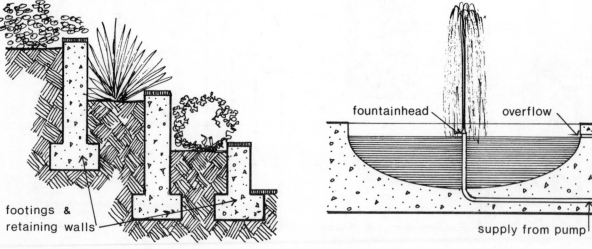

footings &
retaining walls

⑤　TERRACED PLANTERS

fountainhead

overflow

supply from pump

⑥　POOL w/FOUNTAIN

Garden Construction Details

A permanent masonry planter is always handsome in a garden; this one holds begonias.

two to three inches wider than the width of the masonry wall you are planning). Fill the trench with concrete (this is the foundation or footing). When the concrete footing is dry, lay the brick or stone with mortar. Be sure to lay the blocks or bricks perfectly level; use a carpenter's level as a guide. For added strength, back the wall with mortar plastered against the inside wall (have your helper do this). At the bottom of the unit add pipes (weep holes to carry off excess water). Build the wall to the desired height and then top it with a cap of flagstone strips or concrete.

The advantage of dry-wall construction is that freezing and thawing will not bother the wall and no footing is required. You can attempt this wall too if there is a helper to handle the stones. Place heavy stones flat side down and lay them with a slight tilt toward the planter bed. Use the heaviest stones at the base of the wall;

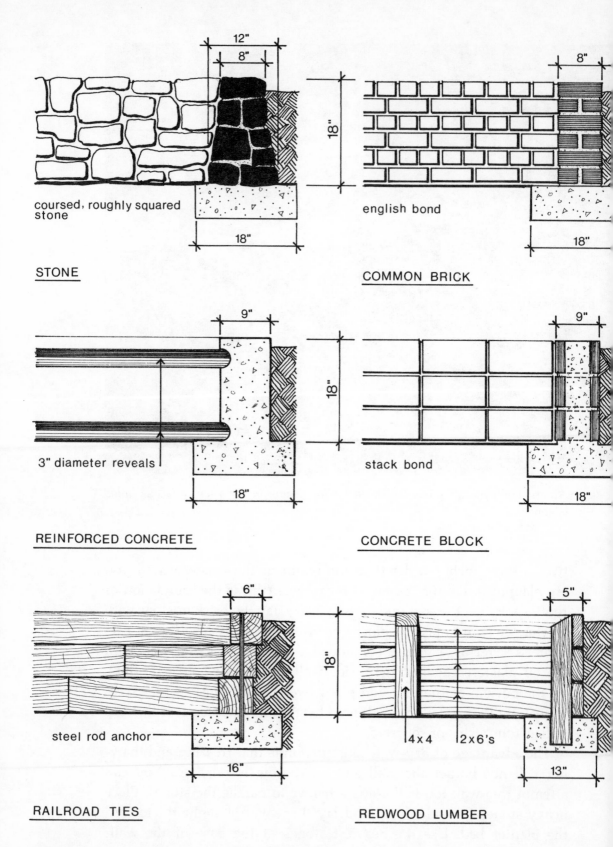

12"

8"

18"

coursed, roughly squared stone

18"

STONE

8"

english bond

18"

COMMON BRICK

9"

18"

3" diameter reveals

18"

REINFORCED CONCRETE

9"

18"

stack bond

18"

CONCRETE BLOCK

6"

steel rod anchor

16"

RAILROAD TIES

5"

18"

4 x 4   2 x 6's

13"

REDWOOD LUMBER

Raised Planter Beds

patiently lay each stone by tamping soil firmly back of the stones as the height of the wall grows. Use smaller stones at the top to form a level finish. There is no need to worry about drainage because excess water will drain from between the stones.

WINDOW BOXES

Today many new versions of the old-fashioned window boxes are available. Like the wooden planters, these planters, which are easy to build, can be a boon for the gardener who prefers standing while working rather than squatting. Although the basic purpose of window boxes was for window adornment, they can also be used on fences, sides of buildings, and so forth in a variety of arrangements, all depending on space. Properly designed and cleverly placed window-type boxes can add dimension and eye interest to a garden when used in tier or grid fashion against a wall or fence. Indeed, they are handsome additions in any area.

All kinds of materials—concrete, metal, plastic—are being used for window boxes, but to me the old-fashioned box is still the best. Redwood resists decay and weathers well (it turns a lovely silver color), and after trying other woods, it certainly was my choice. Leave the outside of the box in its natural finish or paint it a contrasting color to match house or fence walls. The size of the area where the box will be dictates the size of the box. However, beware of very long window boxes; they become too heavy when filled with soil, and hanging them properly can be a problem. Two small ones would be better than one very large one. The most satisfactory dimensions are a width of ten inches, a depth of twelve inches, and a length of twenty-eight to thirty-six inches.

Because window boxes are heavy (a five-foot box filled with soil weighs about four hundred pounds) they must be securely fastened to the building wall. Bolt them to wall studs or fasten them with lag screws. In addition, I install sturdy L-shaped iron brackets for support.

If your outdoor season is short, don't plant directly into the box; merely set potted plants inside it. Fill in and around the pots with peat moss or sphagnum. There are two advantages to this method: (1) it is easy to move plants into the house when cool weather starts, and (2) it isn't necessary to buy additional soil. Where winters are severe, protect window boxes or they may crack. Remove the soil from them, and cover the boxes with tarpaulin or plastic cloth or fill them with potted evergreens in winter.

The idea of window-box gardening is a sound one. Plants are exposed to the circulation of air on all sides, they benefit from rain, and they have ample soil to grow in. Soil dries out rapidly in flower boxes, so water frequently, sometimes twice a day in July and August. Use a general greenhouse soil for the boxes, and a month after planting start a regular feeding program as you do for house plants. Almost any kind of a plant can be grown in a window box; the following lists will give you some starters.

This unique variation of window boxes is extremely attractive and so easy to tend plants in. (Larsen photographs; Courtesy California Redwood Assoc.)

For Full Sun
  Geranium
  Lantana
  Lobelia
  Nasturtium
  Petunia

For Partial Sun
  Browallia
  Heliotrope
  Impatiens
  Begonia semperflorens

For Partial Shade
  Aeschynanthus
  Episcia
  Fuchsia
  Tuberous begonia
  Achimenes

Vines and Trailers
  Bougainvillea
  Cobaea scandens
  Thunbergia alata
  Tuberous begonias (pendula type)

PREPARING PLANTER BEDS

Provide a porous soil for plants in masonry or wooden planters. Planters take money and time, especially if you have had them built, so it is senseless to have poor soil that will lead to ugly, dying plants.

Before you add fresh soil to a permanent planter, loosen the sub-soil on which the box rests; do this with a small fork or hand cultivator. If soil is caked, water can't penetrate it, and all your work will be for nothing. Add some humus and compost and work it into the existing soil. Install a bed of crushed rock or gravel to facilitate drainage. Now add new soil to within two inches of the top of the planter, for easy watering.

Sun, hot air, and wind cause soil in planters to dry out rapidly, so if there isn't ample rainfall be sure to water plants copiously, especially during hot months. Water deeply and heavily. Keep weeds out of planters; once the planter is established and plants are growing strong, weeds will seldom appear, but until then watch for stray weeds and remove them. Every other week during spring and summer add some plant food to the soil. Use a general fertilizer such as 10-10-5. (Granular form is the easiest; just sprinkle it on the soil and water.)

In winter plants need protection from severe weather, so cover them with a thin mulch, or in the case of evergreens, be sure they get some attention.

Working with wood allows great versatility; this pyramid garden is functional and beautiful. Plants are succulents but almost any plant could be grown in the planter bins. (Photo by Ken Molino for California Redwood Assoc.)

Pyramid Gardens

Be daring with your no-bend gardens; a fine example is shown in the photograph of a pyramid design resplendent with succulents. This garden looks complicated, but it is simple to build, offers great beauty for little work, and the plants in it are very easy to care for. Planting pockets are wide enough to accommodate many kinds of plants, and the design of the planter provides shade and sun so plants are not always in intense sun. Make shelves at least ten to twelve inches deep and seven to eight inches wide for maximum use, and construct the planter from redwood.

This garden can be placed anywhere on the property for accent or may be used as the garden itself—fill planting pockets with rich soil and put plants in place. Our photograph shows succulents, but all kinds of plants can be used with equal success. The pyramid unit is ideal for annuals and perennials, vegetables, etc.

Pole-and-Post Floating Gardens

Pole-and-post gardens may not strike you as real gardens when you first think of them. However, this no-bend kind of gardening really offers unlimited ways of growing plants in pots, and at waist and eye levels they make dramatic viewing. Commercial poles and containers are available from suppliers, but you can make your own designs with 4 x 4-inch posts either anchored into the ground in concrete or to wood decks with L-shaped brackets.

The purpose of this garden in the air is not only to avoid bending

Pot-and-post gardens put plants at waist level, easy to reach and to view. (Photo courtesy Architectural Pottery Co.)

when tending plants but also to achieve dimension and drama. Bolt pots with holes in the bottom to posts and anchor the posts to the ground (as mentioned above). The construction is so simple that in one afternoon you can have an attractive garden.

Place the containers—anything from clay pots to architectural bowls—one to a post, at varying heights to create constant interest. However, don't set them so high you can't easily reach plants. If possible, use three or five in a group for a pleasing arrangement. Try to use the same kind of container for each group. If you want, add pots to the post sides to create a tier garden, but avoid overloading the post. Simple pot hangers that clip on to the edge of standard clay pots are available for this arrangement.

You can grow almost anything, from annuals and perennials to vegetables and herbs, in this floating garden. (Trees and shrubs are of course beyond the post garden idea.) Use trailing plants and upright growers, and strive for an ideal arrangement. We grow ferns and trailers such as chlorophytum; they are stunning in such a situation, the entire plant can be seen, and they grow lavishly because foliage is never bruised. Cascading petunias and fuchsias are other stellar candidates for these unusual gardens, and don't forget upright plants such as asters.

Select an area with ample sun and some wind protection. You are creating a sculptural garden when you work with posts, so it is best to view this scene from a distance rather than close up.

Pot-and-post gardens can be used in many different areas; here they are on a deck, a handsome decorative note. (Joshua Freiwald Photo for California Redwood Assoc.)

6. Special Gardens for the Handicapped ✍

If the rigors of full-time gardening are beyond your capacity there are other kinds of special gardens to give you a chance to work with the soil and enjoy flowers. Growing plants in containers is one way; plants in stone or concrete trays is another way. And too, there are special gardens for the people confined to a wheelchair. Gardening is really for everyone! It is just a question of the kind of garden to suit your needs and capacity.

Container Gardens

Plants in pots or ornamental containers are always decorative and scores of people use them. Container gardens are also well suited to people with minor handicaps for it offers a way to garden without too much work. The arrangement of the garden is up to you and if one plant doesn't work it is easy to move it to another place until a satisfying scheme is achieved.

Small or large containers—wood or clay—can be used depending on just what you want. They may be grouped together or you can have modular wooden planters in different arrangements. The container garden can be an everchanging landscape—using seasonal plants through spring, summer, and fall.

Almost any plant can be grown in containers: annuals, perennials, bulbs, small trees and shrubs. Even vegetables can be grown in con-

In this photo, a hanging container garden affords decorative plants for a patio. (Roger Scharmer photo)

57

This small container garden offers beauty and a chance for the lesser agile gardener to keep his fingers in the dirt. (Photo by Roger Scharmer)

tainers if that is your preference. The main thing is to arrange the containers in pleasing groups rather than just an isolated pot here or there. And do seek ornamental tubs and jardinieres to make the garden unique.

In winter, move plants indoors to enjoy them on gray days. Come spring put them outside to decorate your patio or garden. Maintenance, after initial planting, is simple: frequent waterings and light feeding of plants. And, again let me mention that flowering plants such as annuals and perennials will need much sun.

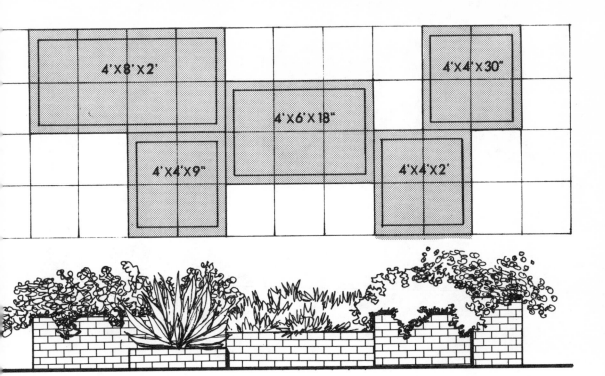

4'X8'X2'

4'X4'X30"

4'X6'X18"

4'X4'X9"

4'X4'X2'

RECTANGULAR PLANTERS

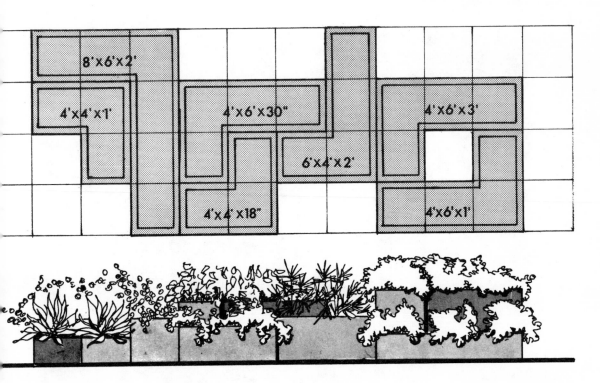

8'X6'X2'

4'X4'X1'

4'X6'X30"

4'X6'X3'

6'X4'X2'

4'X4'X18"

4'X6'X1'

L-SHAPED PLANTERS

Modular Planters

A delightful scene is this container garden, easy to tend, lovely to see. (Roger Scharmer photo)

A pot garden of bulbs on a stairway lends charm and color to this area. (Hort Pix photo)

Remember that container gardening makes it possible for you to do as much or as little as you please, and the garden can be as small or as large as you think you can manage. A small vegetable garden keeps work to a minimum and provides a maximum harvest.

WHEELCHAIR GARDENS

A garden with properly planned paths can be used by wheelchair gardeners, but make the paths wide and smooth for easy locomotion. Plywood boards are suitable for the paths and can be easily installed by a handyman. Remember that beds and borders can't be too wide because for easy cultivation you must have access from both sides.

A wheelchair gardener with lots of vigor. The garden is always colorful and a joy to see. (Photo courtesy Independent Journal Newspaper)

Don't make the garden too large, but do plant it so it is attractive. Of course the garden will have to be dug and planted, but once it is established the wheelchair gardener can find considerable work to keep him active in all seasons but winter. There will be enough to do but not so much that gardening becomes tiresome. Incorporate as many raised beds as possible (see Chapter 5) for easy gardening, and use container plants as accents. You can even grow small trees in suitable containers for garden decoration.

Use modern tools to work the garden; an invaluable tool is a light push-pull type of hoe with a long handle. Other similarly designed tools are also available from suppliers, or make your own.

STONE OR TRAY GARDENS

I see more and more of this type of gardening. Miniature gardens in sinks, troughs, etc. offer a wonderful outlet for people who want to exercise their creative sense and keep their fingers and mind busy.

Note the three-pronged weeder this armchair gardener uses. (Photo courtesy Independent Journal Newspaper)

Stone tray gardening is a delightful hobby and an easy way to grow lovely miniature plants. (Photo by Roy Elliot)

The sink garden is a fine place to grow alpines and rock garden plants, and more charming flowers are difficult to find. They are not easy to grow, however, but the bounty of bloom is well worth the challenge.

Concrete sinks and troughs are hard to find but concrete birdbaths and stone containers are available, and if they are four to six inches deep, they can be used. Even terra cotta drip saucers (now available in large sizes and depths) can be sink gardens, or you can make your own concrete containers. Whatever you use, be sure it has plenty of drainage holes in the bottom and is strong, weather resistant, and deep enough to hold small trees or shrubs.

The big advantage of sink gardening is that at waist level it eliminates stooping and squatting. And, too, the garden is elevated and easy to see and can be placed almost anywhere on the property, although a protected place with half sun is preferred. Use bricks, concrete blocks, or pedestal posts to support the miniature landscape.

Start the sink garden by covering the bottom of the container with about a half inch of small stones. Then add a thin layer of moist peat moss. Now add soil to about one-third the depth of the container. Press the soil in place to eliminate air pockets, and shape the soil in attractive hills and valleys for eye interest. Do not immediately plant—first move the potted plants around in the garden until you find the right place for them. Then remove them from their pots with as much root ball intact as possible and plant. Add gravel paths, small stones, and other decorations to make the setting handsome.

A sink garden is heavy when filled with soil and plants, so remember to assemble it in a permanent place. These gardens are essentially for the outdoors, but some can be grown in an unheated but not freezing room where there is ample light. In winter outdoors most gardens will need some protection from weather. Cover them with oak leaves, hay, or straw, as you would mulch a regular garden.

Watering depends on the weather and the kind of plants being grown as well as the soil mix and size of the garden. Buy plants from mail-order suppliers who specialize in rock garden and alpine species.

7. Stocking the Garden ♫

The garden will glow if you plant vibrantly colored annuals and perennials. Although there may be difficult kinds there are an equal number of easy ones that require only sowing to put the garden in a festive mood. Trees and shrubs, the backbone of a good garden, can be easily installed too. But remember that planting time—spring or fall—is as important as selection. Fortunately, however, even if you go wrong in selecting the right season for planting, most trees and shrubs will survive provided they are suitable for your climate zone.

ANNUALS AND PERENNIALS

Annuals produce flowers, mature, and then die in one season. They can be either grown from seed or purchased cheaply at the correct season and merely set into the ground with little trouble. However, with this latter method you must bend, whereas with seeds you merely stand and scatter. Most annuals are prolific bloomers that require little more than sun and water, but don't forget that annuals flower only once, so you'll need other plants if you want continual color.

A perennial is a plant that generally blooms the second year after it is planted and thrives for many seasons. Thus, if you plant perennials you'll have color for several years. Buy seedlings at nurseries or grow your own from seed.

Be sure to put both annuals and perennials where they will receive plenty of sun or bloom will be sparse. Water them frequently and long because these plants need good moisture to really thrive. Following is a list of some of the most popular annuals and perennials.

66

ANNUALS

BOTANICAL AND COMMON NAME	APPROX. HEIGHT, INCHES	RANGE OF COLORS	PEAK BLOOMING SEASON	SUN OR SHADE
Antirrhinum majus (common snapdragon)	10 to 48 PD* 10 to 18	Large choice of color and flower form	Late spring and fall; summer where cool	Sun
Arctotis stoechadifolia grandis	16 to 24 PD 10	Yellow, rust, pink, white	Early spring	Sun
Begonia semperflorens (wax begonia)	6 to 18 PD 6 to 8	White, pink, deep-rose; single or double flowers	All summer; perennial in temperate climate	Sun or shade
Calendula officinalis (calendula or pot marigold)	12 to 24 PD 12 to 15	Cream, yellow, orange, apricot	Winter where mild; late spring else-where	Sun
Centaurea cyanus (bachelors button or cornflower)	12 to 30 PD 12	Blue, pink, wine, white	Spring where mild; summer elsewhere	Sun
Clarkia amoena (godetia) (farewell-to-spring)	18 to 30 PD 9	Mostly mixed colors: white, pink, salmon, lavender	Late spring; summer where cold	Sun or shade
Coreopsis tinctoria (calliopsis)	8 to 30 PD 18 to 24	Yellow, orange, maroon, and splashed bicolors	Late spring to summer; late summer where cool	Sun
Delphinium ajacis (rocket larkspur)	18 to 60 PD 9	Blue, pink, lavender, rose, salmon, carmine	Late spring to early summer	Sun
Dianthus species (pinks)	6 to 30 PD 4 to 6	Mostly bicolors of white, pink, lavender, purple	Spring and fall; winters where mild	Sun
Eschscholzia californica (California poppy)	12 to 24 PD 9	Gold, yellow, orange; "Mission Bell" varieties include pink and rose	Winter and spring in mild climates	Sun
Gaillardia pulchella (rose-ring Gaillardia)	12 to 24 PD 9	Zoned patterns in warm shades; wine, maroon	All summer	Sun

Lovely annuals give quick color for the summer but remember they last only one season; these are petunias and snapdragons. (USDA photo)

BOTANICAL AND COMMON NAME	APPROX. HEIGHT, INCHES	RANGE OF COLORS	PEAK BLOOMING SEASON	SUN OR SHADE
Godetia amoena (See *Clarkia amoena*)				
Gypsophila elegans	12 to 30 PD 6	White, rose, pink	Early summer to fall but of short duration	Sun
Helianthus annuus (common garden sunflower)	36 to 120 or more PD 3	Yellow, orange, mahogany, or yellow with black centers	Summer	Sun
Helichrysum bracteatum (strawflower)	24 to 48 PD 9 to 12	Mixed warm shades; yellow, bronze, orange, pink, white	Late summer; fall	Sun
Impatiens balsamina (garden balsam)	8 to 30 PD 9	White, pink, rose, red	Summer to fall	Light shade; sun where cool
Lathyrus odoratus (sweet pea, winter flowering)	36 to 72 PD 6	Mixed or separate colors; all except yellow, orange, and green	Late winter where mild	Sun
Lobelia erinus (edging lobelia)	2 to 6 PD 6 to 8	Blue, violet, pink, white	Summer	Sun, light shade
Lobularia maritima (sweet alyssum)	4 to 12 PD 12	White, purple, lavender, rosy-pink	Year-round where mild; spring to fall elsewhere	Sun, light shade
Mathiola incana (stock)	12 to 36 PD 9 to 12	White, cream, yellow, pink, rose, crimson-red, purple	Winter where mild; late spring elsewhere	Sun
Mirabilis jalapa (four-o-clock)	36 to 48 PD 12	Red, yellow, pink, white; some with markings	All summer	Light shade or full sun
Petunia hybrids	12 to 24 PD 6 to 12	All colors except true blue, yellow, and orange	Summer and fall	Sun

Botanical and common name	Approx. height, inches	Range of colors	Peak blooming season	Sun or shade
Phlox drummondii (annual phlox)	6 to 18 PD 6 to 9	Numerous bicolors; all shades except blue and gold	Late spring to fall	Sun, light shade
Salpiglossis sinuata (painted tongue)	18 to 36 PD 9	Bizarre patterns of red, orange, yellow, pink, purple	Early summer	Sun, light shade
Tagetes erecta (hybrids and species) (big or African marigold)	10 to 48 PD 12 to 18	Mostly yellow, tangerine, and gold	Generally, all summer	Sun
T. patula (hybrids and species) (French marigold)	6 to 18 PD 9	Same as African types; also russet, mahogany, and bicolors	Early summer	Sun
T. tenufolia signata (signet marigold)	10 to 24 PD 9 to 12	Small; yellow, orange	Generally, all summer	Sun
Zinnia angustifolia (Mexican zinnia)	12 to 18 PD 6 to 9	Yellow, orange, white, maroon, mahogany	Summer	Sun
Z. elegans (small-flowered zinnia)	8 to 36 PD 9	Red, orange, yellow, purple, lavender, pink, white	Summer	Sun
Z. elegans (giant-flowered zinnia)	12 to 36 PD 12	Same colors as small-flowered zinnia	Summer	Sun

*PD = planting distance.

Flowering annuals and perennials frame this lovely small terrace. (Photo by Roger Scharmer)

PERENNIALS

Botanical and common name	Approx. height, inches	Range of colors	Peak blooming season	Sun or shade
Althea rosea (hollyhock)	60 to 108	Most colors except true blue and green	Summer	Sun
Alyssum saxatile (basket of gold)	8 to 12	Golden-yellow, tinged with chartreuse	Early spring	Sun
Anemone coronaria (poppy-flowered anemone)	To 18	Red, blue, white	Spring	Sun
Asclepsis tuberosa (butterfly weed)	24 to 36	Orange	Summer	Sun
Aster, dwarf type	8 to 15	Red, blue, purple	Late summer	Sun
Campanula carpatica (tussock bellflower)	8 to 10	Blue, white	Summer	Sun
C. persicifolia (willow bellflower)	24 to 36	White, blue, pink	Summer	Sun
Chrysanthemum coccineum (Pyrethrum) (painted daisy)	24 to 36	White, pink, red	Early summer	Sun
C. maximum (Daisy chrysanthemum)	24 to 48	White	Summer, fall	Sun or shade
C. morifolium (florists chrysanthemum)	18 to 30	Most colors except blue	Late summer, fall	Sun
Convallaria majalis (lily-of-the-valley)	9 to 12	White, pink	Spring, early summer	Light to medium shade
Coreopsis grandiflora	24 to 36	Golden yellow	Summer	Sun
Delphinium hybrid (Connecticut Yankee)	24 to 36	Blue, violet, white	Early summer	Sun
Dianthus barbatus (sweet William)	10 to 30	White, pink, red; zoned and edged	Early summer	Sun or light shade
Felicia amelloides (blue daisy)	20 to 24	Blue	Spring, summer	Sun
Gaillardia grandiflora (blanket flower)	24 to 48	Yellow or bicolor	Summer, fall	Sun

Botanical and common name	Approx. height, inches	Range of colors	Peak blooming season	Sun or shade
Gazania hybrids	10 to 12	Yellow and brown bicolors	Summer, fall, spring where mild	Sun
Gypsophila paniculata (baby's breath)	24 to 36	White	Early summer and summer	Sun
Helenium (various) (sneezeweed)	24 to 48	Orange, yellow, rusty shades	Summer, fall	Sun
Hemerocallis (various) (day lily)	12 to 72	Most colors except blue, green, violet	Midsummer	Sun or light shade
Hosta plantaginea (fragrant plantain lily)	24 to 30	White flowers, yellow-green leaves	Late summer	Light shade
Iris (various) (bearded iris)	3 to 10 (dwarf); 15 to 28 (intermediate); 24 to 48 (tall)	Many, many colors	Spring, early summer	Sun or light shade
Iris cristata (crested iris)	6 to 8	Lavender, light blue	Spring	Light shade
Kniphofia (various) (torch lily)	24 to 72	Cream, white, yellow, orange	Early summer	Sun
Liatris pycnostachya (gayfeather)	60 to 72	Rose-purple	Summer	Sun or light shade
Lobelia cardinalis (Cardinal flower) (Indian pink)	24 to 36	Red	Late summer	Sun, light shade
Rudbeckia hirta (black-eyed Susan)	36 to 48	Yellow, pink, orange, white	Summer	Sun
Salvia patens (blue salvia sage) (gentian sage)	24 to 36	Dark blue	Summer, fall	Sun
Scabiosa caucasica (pincushion flower)	24 to 30	White, blue, purple	Summer, fall	Sun
Solidago (various) (goldenrod)	20 to 36	Yellow	Summer	Sun or light shade
Veronica (various) (speedwell)	24 to 36	Blue, pink, white	Midsummer	Light shade

Botanical and common name	Approx. height, inches	Range of colors	Peak blooming season	Sun or shade
Viola cornuta (horned viper)	6 to 8	Purple; newer varieties in many colors	Spring, fall	Light shade
Yucca filamentosa (Adam's needle)	36 to 72	White	Late summer	Sun

TREES

Trees are a necessary part of any attractive garden, so don't be hesitant about using some (but not so many that the garden becomes a totally shaded place where nothing else will grow). And don't be afraid to plant seedlings because you think they won't grow while your're alive—like children, trees grow before you know it. Furthermore, there *are* fast-growing trees, and smaller trees are good choices too because they don't take too long to mature. There are trees for all situations, and your local nurseryman can help you select trees for your area, but first know something about trees so you can talk intelligently with him.

First of all, you want a tree that will do well; leave experimenting to the young gardeners. Stick with old favorites and standbys that are reliable performers. Decide whether you want: year-round or seasonal flowers, tall shade trees or small trees near a terrace, or, colorful foliage in fall, or an evergreen for year-round beauty. After you decide on those factors, remember these four planning rules:

1. The tree must be in proportion to the other landscape material and to the size of the house.
2. Be sure the shape of the tree—mushroom, canopy, columnar—harmonizes with other planting materials.
3. Fit the tree to the best location.
4. Select the major shade trees first and then add the other trees that you want.

CARE AND PLANTING

The best tree to buy is young, dormant, and deciduous and ready to grow. As discussed in Chapter 3, trees at your nursery will be either balled and burlapped or in cans. No matter which you select, study it first to be sure it is the kind you want. Don't make snap decisions; look at many trees before making a final purchase.

Make the planting hole deep, about twice the size of the diameter of the root ball and at least half again as deep as the height of the root ball. Put a mound of soil in the bottom of the hole, and place the plant on it so that the crown is slightly above the soil line. Pour in water and let the soil settle. Next, fill the hole to the top with soil and form a water well around the plant. Soak, fill the well a few times, and allow water to penetrate the soil. When you think you have added enough water, add some more.

For bare-root trees, follow the above planting suggestions and spread out roots; never bend, cut, or squeeze the roots into the hole. Follow the same procedure for plants from cans but leave the root ball; be sure to leave the burlap on the tree roots with B&B tree—cut it when the tree is in the soil. (The burlap will decay in time.)

Once trees are growing they will need pruning at specific times of the year, in addition to watering. You can, of course, do some pruning yourself, but basically it pays to call in a professional. If you prune plants be sure to follow these hints:

Remove Y-shaped crotches by cutting away the smaller of the two branches to stimulate the growth of the remaining branch and strengthen the wood.

Shape trees as they are growing instead of waiting several years; drastic pruning (difficult work) will hurt both the tree and you.

Stake trees with guy wires if necessary; a crooked tree is not pleasant to look at.

Overgrown mature trees will need daylighting: thin and remove small branches so light can reach all parts of the tree. (Warning: this is strictly work for a professional.)

Generally spring is the best time to feed a tree—feed every other watering with a mild fertilizer for about a month; later feeding is really not needed.

Here is a table of some deciduous and evergreen trees for your garden.

DECIDUOUS TREES

Botanical and Common Name	Approx. Height, Feet	Minimum Night Temp.	Remarks
Acer platanoides (Norway maple)	90	−35° to −20° F.	Grows rapidly
A. rubrum (red maple)	120	−35° to −20° F.	Best show in late spring
Aesculus carnea (red horse chestnut)	60	−35° to −20° F.	No autumn color
Ailanthus altissima (tree of heaven)	60	−20° to −10° F.	Very adaptable
Albizzia julibrissin (silk tree)	20	− 5° to −10° F.	Very ornamental
Betula pendula (European white birch)	60	−40° to −30° F.	Graceful but short lived
Carya ovata (shagbark hickory)	130	−30° to −10° F.	Narrow upright habit
Celtis occidentalis (hackberry)	75	−50° to −35° F.	Good shade tree
Cercis canadensis (eastern redbud)	26	−20° to −10° F.	Lovely flowers
Chionanthus virginica (fringe tree)	20	−20° to −10° F.	Bountiful flowers
Cornus florida (flowering dogwood)	25	−30° to −10° F.	Stellar ornamental
C. kousa (Japanese dogwood)	20	−10° to −5° F.	Lovely flowers in June
Crataegus mollis (downy hawthorn)	30	−20° to −10° F.	Pear-shaped red fruit
Fagus grandifolia (American beech)	120	−35° to −20° F.	Stellar tree
F. sylvatica (European beech)	100	−20° to −10° F.	Several varieties
Fraxinus americana (White ash)	120	−35° to −20° F.	Grows in almost any soil
Gingko biloba (maidenhair tree)	120	−20° to −10° F.	Popular
Gleditsia triacanthos (sweet locust)	100	−20° to −10° F.	Several varieties
Koelreuteria paniculata (goldenrain tree)	30	−10° to −5° F.	Magnificent summer bloom

BOTANICAL AND COMMON NAME	APPROX. HEIGHT, FEET	MINIMUM NIGHT TEMP.	REMARKS
Laburnum watereri (golden chain tree)	25	−10° to −5° F.	Deep-yellow flowers
Liquidambar styraciflua (sweet gum)	90	−10° to −5° F.	Beautiful symmetry
Magnolia soulangeana (saucer magnolia)	25	−10° to −5° F.	Many varieties; also evergreens, shrubs
M. stellata (starry magnolia)	20	−10° to −5° F.	Very ornamental
Malus baccata (Siberian crab apple)	45	−50° to −35° F.	Lovely flowers and fruit
M. floribunda (showy crab apple)	30	−20° to −10° F.	Handsome foliage and flowers
Populus alba (white poplar)	90	−35° to −20° F.	Wide-spreading branches
Salix alba (white willow)	40	−50° to −35° F.	Good upright willow
S. babylonica (weeping willow)	40	−10° to −5° F.	Fast grower
Tilia americana (American linden)	90	−50° to −35° F.	Fragrant white flowers in July
T. cordata (small-leaved linden)	60	−35° to −20° F.	Dense habit
T. tomentosa (silver linden)	80	−20° to −10° F.	Beautiful specimen tree
Ulmus americana (American elm)	100	−50° to −35° F.	Most popular shade tree

EVERGREEN TREES

BOTANICAL AND COMMON NAME	APPROX. HEIGHT, FEET	MINIMUM NIGHT TEMP.	REMARKS
Abies balsamea (balsam fir)	70	−35° to −20° F.	Handsome ornamental
Cedrus atlantica (atlas cedar)	100	−5° to −5° F.	Nice pyramid
Chamaecyparis obtusa (Hinoki cypress)	130	−20° to −10° F.	Broadly pyramidal

An intelligent plan: flowering plants for seasonal color with shrubs and trees as the framework. (Photo by author)

Botanical and common name	Approx. height, feet	Minimum night temp.	Remarks
Cryptomeria japonica "Lobbi"	30 to 50	−5° to −5° F.	Pyramidal shape
Juniperus virginiana (red cedar)	30 to 50	−50° to −35° F.	Slow growing
Picea abies (excelsa) (Norway spruce)	75	−50° to −35° F.	Not for small grounds
Pinus bungeana (lacebark pine)	75	−20° to −10° F.	Slow growing
P. densiflora (Japanese red pine)	80	−20° to −10° F.	Flat-top habit
P. nigra (Austrian pine)	90	−20° to −10° F.	Fast growing
P. parviflora (Japanese white pine)	90	−10° to −5° F.	Handsome ornamental
Taxus baccata (English yew)	60	−5° to 5° F.	Best among yews
T. cuspidata "Capitata" (Japanese yew)	50	−20° to −10° F.	Good landscape tree
Thuja occidentalis (American arborvitae)	65	−50° to −35° F.	Sometimes needles turn brown in winter
Tsuga canadensis (hemlock)	75	−35° to −20° F.	Many uses: hedges, screens, landscapes
T. caroliniana (Carolina hemlock)	75	−20° to −10° F.	Fine all-purpose evergreen
T. diversifolia (Japanese hemlock)	90	−10° to −5° F.	Smaller than most hemlocks

SHRUBS

Shrubs come in many shapes, sizes, and leaf textures, and a certain amount of them are definitely necessary in almost any attractive garden. The deciduous shrubs provide wild splashes of color, and the evergreens supply year-round beauty. The forms of these plants can be spreading, round topped, low, or high. Try to fit the plant to the area so it becomes a total part of the composition; shrubs should be used in broad brush strokes rather than as an accent here or there.

Buying and Planting

Like trees, shrubs are sold B&B, in containers, or bare root. Deciduous types, which lose their leaves in winter, are available during their dormant season, for spring planting. Broad-leaved shrubs and evergreens (narrow-leaved) are available in containers or B&B at planting time.

Dig deep large hole for shrubs, and spread out the roots as you put them in the planting pockets. Break up the soil in the bottom of the hole, and add some topsoil so the plants can prosper. Always set shrubs in the ground at the same level they were at the nursery. Don't bury too much of the trunk below the ground. Spacing shrubs is a touchy subject among gardeners; some put a two-foot shrub about twelve feet from the next shrub. Other gardeners space plants every six feet; I am one of these because I am always anxious for the garden to look complete and lovely.

If you use shrubs in hedges, remember that they will need clipping periodically to keep them attractive. Hedges may be tall or low, deciduous or evergreen, low growing or rigid, clipped or unclipped. For easy maintenance choose natural compact shrubs that are easy to prune; some shrubs will always look shaggy if clipped.

Plant hedge shrubs the way you would regular shrubs, but be sure to get them in a straight line: stretch a string along the spot to be planted, and mark a line on the ground. Plant evergreen hedges in fall or spring and deciduous ones in spring. Don't fertilize hedges too much or you'll have to trim them more frequently.

SHRUBS

Botanical and common name	Approx. height, feet	Minimum Night temp.	Remarks
Abelia grandiflora (glossy abelia)	5	−10° to −5° F.	Free flowering
Abeliophyllum distichum (Korean white forsythia)	3-4	−10° to −5° F.	Prune after bloom

Botanical and common name	Approx. height, feet	Minimum Night temp.	Remarks
Andromeda polifolia (bog rosemary)	1-2	−50° to −35° F.	Likes moist locations
Berberis koreana (Korean barberry)	2-10	−10° to −5° F.	Good outstanding colors; red berries
B. thunbergii (Japanese barberry)	7	−10° to −5° F.	Grows in any soil
Buddleia alternifolia (fountain buddleia)	12	−10° to −5° F.	Graceful; branching
B. davidii (butterfly bush)	15	−10° to −5° F.	Many varieties
Buxus microphylla japonica (Japanese boxwood)	4	−10° to −5° F.	Low and compact
B. microphylla koreana (Korean boxwood)	6-10	−20° to −10° F.	Hardiest; foliage turns brown in winter
Carpenteria californica (California mock orange)	8	5° to 20° F.	Showy shrub
Euonymus alata (winged euonymus)	9	−35° to −20° F.	Sturdy, easily grown
E. japonica (evergreen euonymus)	15	10° to 20° F.	Splendid foliage
E. latifolius	20	−10° to −5° F.	Vigorous grower
Forsythia intermedia (border forsythia)	2-9	−20° to −5° F.	Deep-yellow flowers
Forsythia ovata (early forsythia)	8	−20° to −10° F.	Earliest to bloom and hardiest
Fothergilla major (large fothergilla)	9	−10° to −5° F.	Good flowers and autumn color
Gardenia jasminoides (Cape jasmine)	4-6	10° to 30° F.	Fragrant
Hamamelis vernalis (spring witch hazel)	10	−10° to −5° F.	Early spring blooms
Hydrangea arborescens "Grandiflora" (Hills-of-snow)	3	−20° to −10° F.	Easy culture
Ilex cornuta (Chinese holly)	9	5° to 10° F.	Bright berries, lustrous foliage

BOTANICAL AND COMMON NAME	APPROX. HEIGHT, FEET	MINIMUM NIGHT TEMP.	REMARKS
Ilex crenata (Japanese holly)	20	−5° to 5° F.	Another good holly
Jasminum nudiflorum (winter jasmine)	15	−10° to −5° F.	Viny shrub, not fragrant
Jasminum officinale (common white jasmine)	30	5° to 10° F.	Tall-growing
Juniperus chinensis "Pfitzeriana" (Pfitzer juniper)	10	−20° to −10° F.	Popular juniper
Kalmia latifolia (mountain laurel)	30	−20° to −10° F.	Amenable grower
Mahonia aquifolium (Oregon grape)	3-5	−10° to −5° F.	Handsome foliage
Pieris floribunda (mountain andromeda)	5	−20° to −10° F.	Does well in dry soil
Pieris japonica (Japanese andromeda)	9	−10° to −5° F.	Splendid color
Potentilla fruticosa (cinquefoil)	2-5	−50° to −35° F.	Many varieties
Spiraea arguta	6	−20° to −10° F.	Free flowering
S. prunifolia (bridal wreath spiraea)	9	−20° to −10° F.	Turns orange in fall
S. thunbergii (thunberg spiraea)	5	−20° to −10° F.	Arching branches
S. veitchii	12	−10° to −5° F.	Good background, graceful
Syringa villosa (late lilac)	9	−50° to −35° F.	Dense, upright habit
S. vulgaris (common lilac)	20	−35° to −20° F.	Many varieties
Viburnum davidii	3	5° to 10° F.	Handsome leaves
V. dentatum (arrowwood)	15	−50° to −35° F.	Red fall color
V. opulus (European cranberry bush)	12	−35° to −20° F.	Good many varieties
V. prunifolium (black haw)	15	−35° to −20° F.	Good specimen plant
V. sieboldii	30	−20° to −10° F.	Stellar performer

Botanical and common name	Approx. height, feet	Minimum Night temp.	Remarks
V. trilobum (cranberry bush)	12	—50° to —35° F.	Effective in winter
Weigela "Bristol Ruby"	7	—10° to —5° F.	Complex hybrid
Weigela "Bristol Snowflake"	7	—10° to —5° F.	Complex hybrid
Weigela florida	9	—10° to —5° F.	Many available

Bulbs

For easy, no-bend gardening, bulbs are a sheer delight. The plant is already in the bulb and merely needs planting and watering to bring a wealth of color to your garden. The new bulb planters—those

Ranunculus are handsome bulb plants for seasonal color in the garden . . . and easy to grow. (Photo by author)

with long handles—eliminate bending and there is no pruning, weeding, or battle with bugs when you plant bulbs.

Many of the most beautiful bulb flowers are winter hardy and thus can be left in the ground year after year; they need cold weather to grow. Other bulbs must be planted and lifted each year— these are the ones to avoid because uprooting and replanting means additional labor in early spring when there are so many other gardening chores to do. But although we shall list the winter-hardy bulbs here, those with more energy and youth can certainly grow the other bulbs also.

PLANTING

Generally, most bulbs need a moisture-retentive and rapid-draining soil of high organic matter. Dig round holes with a concave bottom because pointed holes leave an air pocket below the bulb. Some confusion exists about which end of the bulb to put into the ground and how deep to plant it. A three-inch depth means that the bulb has its top, not its bottom, three inches below the ground level. The pointed end of the bulb is usually the one showing growth and therefore the one that goes in the ground. Firm the soil around the bulb rather than leaving it loose.

Buy the best bulbs you can afford from *reputable* dealers. Because you are buying an unseen product you must trust the dealer's reputation rather than your eye.

Bulbs have their own storehouse of food, but they cannot grow indefinitely without some help from you. In active growth be sure to water them regularly, and after flowers have faded continue watering to ripen the next year's growth.

There are hardy spring-flowering bulbs and summer-flowering ones. A list of each type follows.

BULBS
Spring-flowering Bulbs

BOTANICAL AND COMMON NAME	WHEN TO PLANT	DEPTH, INCHES	SUN OR SHADE	REMARKS
Allium (flowering onion)	Fall	3	Sun	Prettier than you think
Crocus	Fall	3	Sun	Always dependable

Botanical and common name	When to plant	Depth, inches	Sun or shade	Remarks
Chionodoxa (glory of snow)	Fall	3	Sun	Do not disturb for several years
Daffodil (jonquil, narcissus)	Fall	6	Sun	The name "daffodil" is used for all members
Eranthis (winter aconite)	Early fall	3	Shade	Very early bloom
Erythronium (dogtooth violet)	Early fall	6	Shade	Good for naturalizing
Fritillaria	Fall	4	Shade	Overlooked but lovely
Galanthus (snowdrop)	Fall	3	Shade	Blooms while snow is on the ground
Hyacinthus (hyacinth)	Fall	6-8	Sun	Protect from wind and mice
Leucojum (snowflake)	Fall	3	Shade	Flowers last a long time
Muscari (grape hyacinth)	Early fall	3	Sun	Easy to grow
Scilla	Fall	2	Sun or light shade	Once established, blooms indefinitely
Tulipa (tulip)	Fall	10-12	Sun	Need cold winters

BULBS
Summer-flowering Bulbs

Botanical and common name	Depth, inches	Sun or shade	Remarks
Agapanthus (flower-of-the-Nile)	1	Sun	New dwarf varieties available
Alstroemeria	4	Sun	Good cut flowers
Begonia (tuberous)	4	Shade	Lovely flowers; many varieties
Canna	2	Sun	Lift bulbs after frost kills tops
Dahlia	3-4	Sun	Need excellent drainage

BOTANICAL AND COMMON NAME	DEPTH, INCHES	SUN OR SHADE	REMARKS
Galtonia (summer hyacinth)	6	Sun	Buy new bulbs yearly
Gladiolus (gladiola)	4-6	Sun	Like copious watering
Iris	4-6	Sun	Many different kinds
Lilium (lily)	4-8	Sun	Best in second year
Polianthus tuberosa (Tuberose)	1	Sun	Plant after danger of frost
Sprekelia formosissima (Jacobean lily)	3	Sun	Good in pots
Ranunculus	1	Sun	Lovely colorful flowers
Tigridia (tiger flower)	2-3	Sun	Plant in early May
Tritonia (montbretia)	2-3	Sun	Plant in early May
Zephyranthes (zephyr lily)	1	Sun or light shade	Plant after danger of frost

8. How to Kill Insects Without Killing Yourself ✐

Years ago, sprays and dusts, chemicals and equipment were part of the gardener's artillery against insect attack, but now there is a better way of combating destructive culprits in the garden: organic gardening. Organic gardening utilizes nature's preventatives, birds and insects, and doesn't involve poisonous chemicals that can kill the good birds and insects along with the bad ones. (And once destroyed, the natural ecology can't be re-established for quite a while). Gardening with nature also involves using natural preventatives such as old-fashioned laundry soap-and-water, and botanical sprays.

ENCOURAGING BIRDS

The most common birds in your garden are liable to be good ones that will keep plants almost insect free. (There are a few birds that will, unfortunately, eat berries and fruits along with their basic diet of insects.) Adult birds also keep their young supplied with insects; at certain times young birds need more than their own weight in food daily.

I bless birds. It's far easier to have the birds control insects than for me to drag out spray cans and apparatus and further contaminate the air with what may be dubious poisons. Birds can be encouraged to visit our gardens if we issue the proper invitation.

ATTRACTING BIRDS

Attract birds with food, protection, bird feeders, and landscaping. (Certain shrubs and trees provide birds with a nesting place and insects to eat.)

Water is also a compelling attraction—birds love to play in it, and in regions where it does not rain for many weeks water for drinking is essential to birds. Birds like shallow or deep bird baths or a mist of water. (You usually don't have to provide water in winter unless there hasn't been any snowfall.)

The following plants help bring birds to the garden:

Shrubs
Bayberry
Blackhaw
Buckthorn
Cranberry
Dogwood
Elderberry
Honeysuckle
Inkberry
Japanese barberry
Winterberry

Vines
Bittersweet
Greenbrier
Hall's honeysuckle
Virginia creeper
Wild grape

Trees
Alder
Ash
Beech
Birch
Flowering crab
Flowering dogwood
Hawthorn
Linden
Maple
Mulberry
Norway spruce
Oak
Red cedar
White spruce

FEEDING BIRDS

Birds also need supplemental feeding to their natural diet of insects. In the summer there is usually enough food for them (unless there is little or no vegetation), but when natural food becomes scarce in winter feeding is essential. Once you start feeding birds you must continue; they rely on you. (There is quite a ruckus on my porch when I forget to feed the birds.)

Select one of the many commercial feeders and locate it close to the house. Insect-eating birds eat much animal matter and their larvae. Avoid suet (a perfect substitute for larvae) so birds will work for their keep. Don't overfeed in the summer.

THE BEST BIRDS

Some birds are better than others for controlling and eating insects: chickadees, house wrens, towhees, and phoebes.

Swallows almost entirely rely on insects for food; the purple martin swallow is perhaps the most useful in the garden. Baltimore orioles eat caterpillars, beetles, ants, grasshoppers, and click beetles, and cuckoos devour hairy caterpillars, beetles, grasshoppers, sawflies, some spiders, tent caterpillars, and crickets. The kingbird is invaluable because he eats almost all kinds of destructive pests. Woodpeckers, although sometimes annoying, eat wood-boring beetles and fruitwood insects; towhees feast on hibernating beetles and larvae. And meadowlarks will also eat some weeds from the lawn as well as bugs.

Avoid certain other birds. Mockingbirds, grosbeaks, and to some extent, members of the sparrow family (e.g. the junco) also eat fruit. The linnet or house finch can be a pest too, and common jays chase away other, more beneficial birds. Helpful birds are:

Baltimore oriole	Kingfisher
Barn swallow	Meadowlark
Brown thrasher	Mockingbird
Catbird	Phoebe
Cedar waxwing	Purple Martin
Downy woodpecker	Song sparrow
Eastern kingbird	Tufted titmouse
House wren	Woodthrush

INSECTS

Some insects are also superb garden protectors. Called predators, they feed on other destructive insects. Ladybugs (beetles) are the most efficient insects. They are veritable aphid-eating machines: the average ladybug (there are about three hundred and fifty species in the United States) can consume four hundred insects a week. The convergent lady beetle is the best suited for insect control because it can be collected in its hibernation state.

If nature hasn't been upset on your property, ladybugs will arrive with the first warm weather. But if you have used chemical sprays you can get ladybugs from suppliers; simply "plant" them in your garden. They come in convenient cases and can be left in their cases for a few days. Place a little water in the box, and put it in the refrigerator. To put ladybugs in the garden, dampen the soil and set them out near food (aphids).

Among the aphis lions (lacewings, ant lions, dobson flies, etc.) the nocturnal lacewings are the best garden controllers; they feed on scale insects, thrips, aphids, mealybugs, moth eggs, and caterpillars. The green lacewing (called golden eyes) and their larvae are both welcome in my garden because they eat aphids, red spiders, and thrips. You can find the larvae of the brown lacewing (called aphis wolves) stuck to the undersides of leaves or on the bark of trees.

Ant lions (doodlebugs) trap their prey by digging a pit, burying themselves at the bottom, and waiting for unwary victims to fall in. Ant lions can destroy quite a number of ants in a single season.

The ambush bug inhabits mainly flowering plants and hides behind foliage or blossoms and then grabs its victims. *Don't* kill these ugly bugs; they have a pair of highly developed front legs that they use for grabbing, and they eat many pests.

The predatory assassin bug, which has a bite as painful as the sting of a wasp, isn't completely beneficial in the garden, but it does have its uses. Damsel bugs are ideal in the garden because they consume aphids, mites, caterpillars, and so forth.

The praying mantises are extremely beneficial and won't leave your property if they have enough insects to eat. When young they eat mainly such soft-bodied insects as aphids and leafhoppers, and when they are mature their diet includes tent caterpillars, chinch bugs, beetles, and other insects.

You can buy egg cases of mantises between November and May. (Figure on about five cases per half acre.) Tie or tape one case to a shrub or tree, at least two to four feet above the ground. The cases will survive during the cold months, and the mantises will emerge sometime in June or July.

Hover flies are quite useful; the larvae of some species feed on aphids, and others love mealybugs and leafhoppers. Tachinid flies are also beneficial because they control caterpillars, cutworms, and armyworms. However, it is difficult to protect these beneficial flies because they look like the ordinary, nonuseful flies.

Spiders belong to the class *Arachnida*, so they aren't true insects—

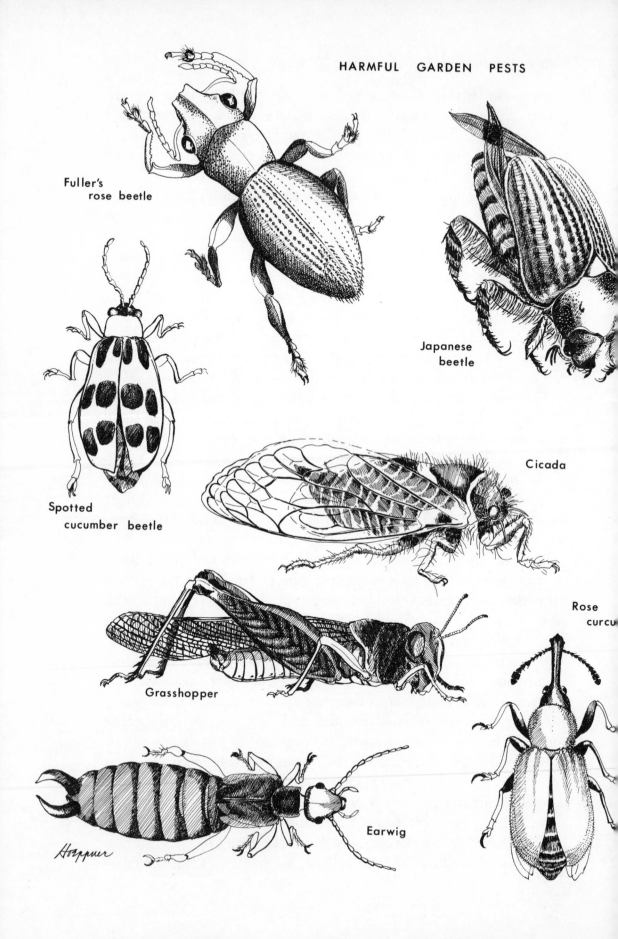

HARMFUL GARDEN PESTS

Fuller's
rose beetle

Japanese
beetle

Spotted
cucumber beetle

Cicada

Rose
curcu

Grasshopper

Earwig

Hoppner

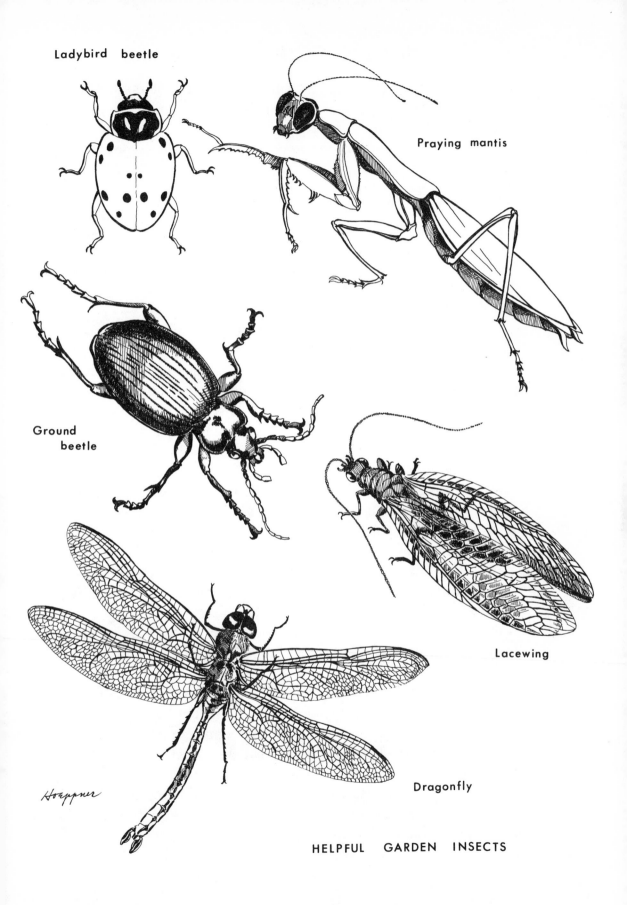

Ladybird beetle

Praying mantis

Ground beetle

Lacewing

Dragonfly

Hoeppner

HELPFUL GARDEN INSECTS

they have four pairs of legs, versus insects' three pairs, and don't have antennae or wings. But many spiders are useful in the garden. In fact, some authorities consider spiders among the dominant predators of the earth. Spiders thrive on live insects. They control pine sawflies and tobacco budworm.

Natural Preventatives

Predatory insects and birds will, to a great extent help to keep the garden generally insect free. But there are other natural defenses that are simple and easy that we can use too. These include companion planting, botanical repellants, and some good old-fashioned remedies that many of us remember.

Any garden with a concentration of one particular plant is an invitation to insects. However, if you mix your plantings or companion-plant, as it is called, there will be a lesser chance of pests invading your garden. Nasturtiums repel aphids and it's a simple matter to scatter some seeds; tansy, a pretty herb, discourages cutworms and cabbageworms. Rue is a hardy evergreen plant that insects will not touch, or as a matter of fact, plants growing near it; marigolds and asters deter insects too, to some degree. But the most popular plants that repel are garlic and chives. Certainly these are easily grown and are not objectionable in the flower garden. Just what is the repellant quality of these plants? With most of them the leaves have a disagreeable odor or a bitter taste. With some it is the color that deters the insects. A prime example of this is orange nasturtiums.

As mentioned, chemical sprays should be avoided in the garden. However, botanical insecticides—pyrethum, rotenone, quassia, and ryania—are not persistent and are not harmful to man or earth. They are botanical repellants made from various plants and are now available as packaged insecticides.

Pyrethum kills on contact aphids, white flies, leafhoppers and thrips. Rotenone wards off spider mite, chinch bug, aphids, and the common housefly. Ryania, although not lethal, incapacitates (perhaps by paralysis) Japanese beetle, elm leaf beetle, and cabbage looper. More and more of the chemical companies that formerly used deadly poisons for garden protection are now marketing these natural repellants. However, check contents on packages carefully to be sure persistent poisons are not added.

Before leaving botanical repellants let us look at a very old one—nicotine—which is available as nicotine sulfate. This is a poisonous alkaloid for insects and it is highly toxic to mammals. However, it dissipates rapidly and is effective against aphids, white fly, leafhopper, and dozens of other pests. If your garden is attacked by a heavy infestation of insects (and this would be rare), occasionally use the nicotine solution if you deem it necessary.

If you can bring yourself to touching insects, whether by foot or hand, hand picking is still an effective way of ridding the small garden of pests. This of course will work for large insects, but for pests such as aphids and spider mites you will have to resort to the old-fashioned solution of laundry soap-and-water. Use a half pound of laundry soap to two gallons of water, spray plants, and then hose them with clear water. This preparation will also eliminate red spider, mealybug, and scale. Don't expect a miracle though, it takes several sprayings to really beat the insects, but it is well worth the trouble in lieu of using poisons.

For more information on natural preventatives see the companion volume in this series, *The Natural Way to Pest-free Gardening*.

A window garden resplendent with choice house plants: begonia and citrus, ferns and aralia. (Photo by Molly Adams)

9. Your Indoor Garden

Indoor gardens—whether on a window sill or in a window box—are our winter retreats, the bridge from fall to spring, and I wouldn't be without house plants. Through the years I have grown an array of indoor beauties, but because outside gardening has occupied me recently and I have tried to cut my gardening—indoors and outdoors —I have eventually eliminated the difficult house plants and concentrated on those that thrive almost by themselves.

I have found that most plants (if given proper light conditions) will respond with lush leaves and bountiful bloom; it is these plants we shall discuss. We won't discuss plants under artificial light because of a lack of space, but this is a fine hobby, and there are many good books about the subject. Those that demand constant attention and are temperamental (e.g. dizygotheca) are too much trouble. I want plants, and I think you might too, that offer the most for least effort.

Minimum Maintenance Plants

A minimum-maintenance house plant is a plant that can grow with nominal watering—about twice a week—and occasional repotting and pruning and still be attractive. Bromeliads of the pineapple family and orchids (yes, orchids) are the plants that can, if necessary, take care of themselves. Bromeliads have built-in vaselike reservoirs that hold water, and orchids have pseudobulbs that see them through drought in case you forget to water them. Ferns and palms are other fine candidates for the gardener who wants a lot for a little care. And agloanemas, begonias, geraniums, and gesneriads are other good plants for the indoor greenery. Cacti and succulents are often overlooked, but they are ideal for indoor decoration and require only an occasional watering in winter.

AVOID THE DIFFICULT PLANTS

It doesn't make much sense to grow difficult plants when there are so many "easy" plants available. Ironically, philodendrons, long classified as excellent house plants, are anything but amenable indoor subjects because they are naturally vining plants not used to confining pots. After a few months they look straggly and must be replaced. Dieffenbachias are other reluctant indoor performers; in the slightest draft they become a disaster area as do the rubber plants and fiddle-leaf fig. In spite of their popularity, African violets are apt to be somewhat fussy too, although newer varieties bred for better bloom and robustness are now appearing.

HOUSE PLANT CULTURE

House plants are either cool growing (60° to 65° F. by day) or warm growing (75° to 80° F. by day). Although plants will tolerate temperature differences, they all need light and won't grow or live without it. Some plants require sun—an east or south window—others need a bright western exposure, and many foliage plants prosper in north light. So select your plants accordingly.

Almost all living rooms provide humidity or air moisture of 30 to 40 percent, which is adequate for most plants. Humidity can be increased in various ways for species requiring more; this is discussed later in the chapter. Fresh air and good ventilation is also essential to plant health, even in very cold weather, but too often plants are relegated to stuffy atmospheres.

POTTING SOILS

I use one-part garden loam to one-part sand to one-part leaf mold for most plants. For cacti and succulents I allow almost one-half instead of one-third sand. Orchids and bromeliads need osmunda (chopped roots of various ferns) or fir bark (steamed pieces of evergreen bark); both can be obtained in small sacks at nurseries.

Commercially packaged soil, usually rather heavy, is good for some plants, particularly African violets and begonias, but not for

An array of fine house plants; three dracaenas in center, Guzmania lingulata, a bromeliad on right. (Photo Architectural Pottery Co.)

all. Usually you can buy a better soil mixture by the bushel from a greenhouse (and this will be the same soil they use). It is sterilized and contains all the necessary ingredients. (Generally, garden soils contain weeds, seeds, insect grubs, and bacteria that can cause disease in plants.) Use it as is, or alter it according to the needs of your own plants. If it is not porous enough, add more sand; if it feels thin, put in more leaf mold or compost.

Growing mediums that contain no soil have been developed by Cornell University, they are called peatlite mixes. For one peck, combine:

> 4 quarts, dry measure, Vermiculite
> 4 quarts, dry measure, shredded peatmoss
> 1 level tablespoon of ground limestone
> 1 level tablespoon 5-10-5 fertilizer

I have found this medium excellent for seedlings, but for tubbed plants you must give supplemental feeding of a water-soluble fertilizer every other watering through the growing season, which is tedious work.

POTTING AND REPOTTING

Potting refers to the first planting of a seeding or cutting in a container; repotting refers to the transfer of a plant from one pot to another, usually larger, one. For good growth; give plants proper potting. Select a container neither too large nor too small in relation to the size of a specimen.

When potting a plant, be sure the container is clean. Soak new clay pots overnight in water before using them or they will draw undue moisture from the soil of new plantings. Scrub old pots with steel-wool soap pads and hot water to remove any algae or salt accumulation.

Fit an arching piece or two of broken pot (shards) over the drainage hole. Over the crocking spread some perlite or porous stones with a few pieces of charcoal (the charcoal keeps the soil sweet). Then place the plant in the center of the pot, and fill in and around it with fresh soil mixture. Hold the plant in position with one hand; fill soil in and around it with the other. Firm soil around the stem with your thumbs. To settle the soil and eliminate air spaces, strike the base of the pot on a table a few times. A properly potted plant can be lifted by the stem without being loosened.

Leave about an inch of space at the top between pot rim and soil so the plant can receive water. Water newly potted plants thoroughly, and then for a few days keep them in a light but not a sunny place. Once accustomed to brightness they can be moved. Label all plants; it's nice to know what you're growing.

It is time to give roots more room and to replenish the soil when roots push through the drainage hole of a pot or appear on the surface. An exact schedule for repotting is not possible; instead, consider the needs of each plant. If you fertilize regularly, thus replacing soil nutrients, plants thrive in the same pot longer than if they are not fed.

WATERING AND FEEDING

How and when you water depends on the type of pot used, where you live, and the kind of plant. Never allow any plant to go completely dry (even during semidormancy), and never keep one in soggy soil. If soil is too dry, plant roots become dehydrated and growth stops; continuously wet soil becomes sour and roots rot.

Some plants prefer an evenly moist soil, but others, like begonias

Orchids are easier to grow than most people realize; this is Dendrobium pierardi with lavender-pink flowers. (Photo by author)

and clivias, grow best in soil that is allowed to approach dryness between waterings. Cacti and some other succulents may be permitted to become almost completely dry.

Water *thoroughly*. Allow excess water to pour from the drainage hole; the complete root system needs moisture. If only the top soil gets wet and the lower part stays dry, the soil usually turns sour and growth is retarded.

Water at room temperature is best. If possible, water in the morning so the soil can dry out before evening. Lingering moisture and cool nights are an invitation to fungus diseases.

Most plants benefit from feeding; however, bromeliads and such flowering plants as many orchids and clerodendrum do not need it. Commercial fertilizers contain some nitrogen, an element that stimulates foliage growth, but too much can retard development of flower buds. Fertilizers also contain phosphorus, which promotes root and stem development and stimulates bloom; and potash, which promotes health, stabilizes growth, and intensifies color. The ratio of elements is marked on the package or bottle in this order: nitrogen, phosphorus, potash. There are many formulas; I prefer 10-10-5 for most house plants.

New and ailing plants do not require feeding. New ones in fresh soil have adequate nutrients and do not need more; ailing plants are not capable of absorbing nutrients. After they flower, allow plants to rest for a few weeks; water only occasionally and do not feed. A safe rule is to fertilize only the plants that are in active growth.

HEAT AND HUMIDITY

Plants like campanulas and hoyas prefer coolness (54° to 58° F. at night, 10° to 15° F. more during the day). Warm-growers like anthuriums and most begonias require 64° to 68° F. at night, 72° to 80° F. during the day. With few exceptions (indicated in the plant list at the end of the chapter), most plants fall into one of these groups. In other words, average home temperatures suit most plants.

In winter it's necessary to protect plants from extreme cold. Put cardboard or newspapers between plants and windows to mitigate the chill of the glass on very cold nights.

Although automatic humidifiers are now part of many heating systems, older apartment houses and buildings don't have them.

Easy house plants include Bromeliads (left and right) and a peperomia (center).
(USDA photo)

Humidity—the amount of moisture in the air—should be at a health-ful level for both people and plants. A humidity gauge (a hygrometer) registers the amount of relative humidity. Thirty to 40 percent is average for most homes and good for most plants. However, some plants, such as clivia and philodendron, will grow in a low humidity, of, say, 30 percent; other plants, like rechsteinerias and gloxinias, require humidity of 60 to 70 percent.

It is hard to keep humidity in the proper relation to artificial and summer heat. The hotter it is, the faster air dries out. Because plants take up water through roots and release it through leaves, they give off moisture faster when the surrounding air is dry rather than damp. If plants use water quicker than they can replace it, foliage becomes thin and depleted. When summer heat is at its peak (between 11:00 A.M. and 1:00 P.M.), spray plants lightly with water. For years, a 15-cent window-cleaning bottle was essential equipment for me, but today's new sprayers give better misting than my old-fashioned gadget. Made under various trade names, these hand-operated fog makers have a plastic, noncorrosive, washable container and come in sixteen- or thirty-two-ounce sizes. They dispense a fine mist that is beneficial to almost all plants, because they cleanse the foliage and, for a brief time anyway, increase the humidity.

In winter, when artificial heat is high (between 8:00 A.M. and 8:00 P.M.), provide more air moisture. Turn on your room humidifier or mist pots and soil surface but not foliage; at night wet foliage is is an invitation to disease.

In addition to misting, set plants on wet gravel in, say, a three-inch-deep large metal or fiberglass tray. This furnishes a good amount of additional humidity. You can also place plants on pebble-filled saucers; keep stones constantly moist. But for best results, use an inexpensive space-humidifier that operates on a small motor; it breaks water into minute particles and diffuses it through the atmosphere.

Strong growth and firm leaves (assuming temperature and light are in proper proportion) are signs of good humidity. Spindly growth and limp leaves usually indicate too little moisture in the air. Keep plants away from hot radiators and blasts of hot air and out of drafts.

IDEAL HOUSE PLANTS

Plant	Size	Time of bloom	Summer outdoors	Exposure	Remarks
Acalypha hispida (chenille plant)	S	May		S	Temporary plant
Aechmea angustifolia	M	Feb.–May	*	L	Blue berries
A. calyculata	M	Nov.–Mar.	*	Sh	Pot offshoots when three inches high

PLANT	SIZE	TIME OF BLOOM	SUMMER OUTDOORS	EXPOSURE	REMARKS
A. chantinii	L	Mar.–June	*	L	Perhaps the best
A. fasciata	M	Sept.–Jan.	*	Sh	Stays colorful for six months
Aeschynanthus specious	V	June–Aug.		L	Keep pot bound
Aglaonema commutatum	M	Dec.		Sh	Avoid repotting; top-dress
Allophyton mexicanum	S	Sept.	*	S	Worth a try
Anthurium scherzerianum	S	Jan.–Apr.		Sh	Grow warm with humidity
Aphelandra aurantiaca Roezlii	S	June		L	Needs good air circulation
Asparagus sprengeri	L	Jan.		Sh	Spray foliage with water frequently
Begonia alleryi	S	Nov.–Mar.		L	Easy to grow
B. "Bow-Arriola"	S	Jan.		L	Grow quite dry
B. "Elsie M. Frey"	V	Oct.		L	Basket type
B. "Limminghei"	V	Jan.–May		L	Grow warm
B. ricinifolia	M	May–Aug.		L	Robust plant
Beloperone guttata (shrimp plant)	M	Oct.–Nov.	*	L	Prune in spring
Billbergia nutans	L	Jan.	*	S	Grow as specimen
Brassavola nodosa	S	Sept.–Oct.		S	Dry out in August
Capsicum annuum	S	Nov.		S	The pepper plant
Ceropegia barklyi	V	Nov.–Dec.		L	Somewhat difficult
C. woodii	V	Dec.		L	Keep on dry side
Chlorophytum elatum	L	Jan.		Sh	Stands abuse
Clerodendrum thomsoniae	L	June		L	Best of group
Clivia miniata	L	Apr.		Sh	Grow quite dry for bloom

Plant	Size	Time of bloom	Summer outdoors	Exposure	Remarks
Coelogyne cristata	S	Feb.		L	Grow cool in November
Columnea arguta	V	Apr.–July		L	Keep in small pots
C. hirta	V	Apr.–July		L	Keep in small pots
Costus igneus	S	July–Aug.		L	A real beauty
Crossandra infundibuliformis	M	Apr.–Aug.		L	Requires good air circulation
Dendrobium pierardii	M	Mar.–May		L	Keep somewhat dry after bloom
Dipladenia amoena	M	June		L	Short rest after flowering
Episcia cupreata	V	July.–Aug.		L	At best in baskets
E. lilacina	V	July.–Aug.		L	At best in baskets
Eucharis grandiflora (Amazon lily)	M	Apr.	*	L	Watch for mealybugs
Eucomis punctata (*comosa*) (pineapple flower)	M	July–Aug.	*	S	Grows from bulb
Euphorbia pulcherrima (poinsettia)	L	Dec.–Jan.		L	The Christmas poinsettia
E. splendens (crown of thorns)	S	Feb.–Apr.	*	L	Grow on the dry side
Gloriosa rothschildiana	V	July–Aug.	*	Sh	Popular tuber plant
Gloxinia (Sinningia)	M	June		L	Keep foliage dry
Hoya bella (wax plant)	V	Sept.–Oct.		Sh	Popular wax plant, miniature form

This attractive house plant corner includes schefflera, ivy and aphelandra. (Photo by Hedrich Blessing)

Plant	Size	Time of bloom	Summer outdoors	Exposure	Remarks
Kaempferia roscoeana	S	June		L	A flower a day in summer
Kalanchoe blossfeldiana	M	Dec.		S	Grow quite dry
Kohleria amabilis	S	June	*	L	Warmth and humidity
K. bogotensis	M	July	*	L	Warmth and humidity
Lantana montevidensis	V	Feb.–Apr.		L	Superior basket plant
Lycaste aromatica	M	Oct.–Nov.		Sh	Dry out severely after flowering
Manettia bicolor	S	Jan.–Mar.		L	Keep potbound
Medinilla magnifica	L	Jan.	*	L	Only mature plants bloom
Musa nana (dwarf banana)	L	Mar.	*	Sh	Pot up offshoots
Neoregelia carolinae	L	Oct.–Feb.	*	Sh	Color for seven months
Nerium oleander	M	June	*	L	Leaves poisonous
Plumbago capensis	L	July–Aug.	*	L	Grow somewhat dry for bloom
Punica granatum "Nana"	S	Oct.		L	Good year-round plant
Rechsteineria leucotricha	S	July–Aug.		S	Rest after flowering
Rhipsalis burchelli	M	Jan.		S	Humidity and warmth
Ruellia macrantha	M	Nov.–Jan.	*	Sh	Bushy
Solanum pseudocapsicum (Jerusalem cherry)	S	Dec.		S	Temporary house plant
Sprekelia formosissima	M	Apr.	*	S	Grow crowded
Stephanotis floribunda (Madagascar jasmine)	V	Apr.	*	L	Give winter rest
Streptocarpus rexii	M	Apr.–July		Sh	Water carefully in winter

PLANT	SIZE	TIME OF BLOOM	SUMMER OUTDOORS	EXPOSURE	REMARKS
Tibouchina semide-candra	S	May–Sept.	*	S	Prune and pinch
Vallota speciosa	M	May		S	Grow dry after flowering
Veltheima viridifolia	L	Dec.		S	Grow dry after flowering

S (small): to twenty-four inches.
M (medium): twenty-four to thirty-six inches.
L (large): thirty-six inches and over.
V vine.

* On porch or in garden for best results.

S (sun): three to four hours.
L (bright light): two or three hours.
Sh (semishade): one to two hours.

10. Greenhouses ✍

Greenhouses are not necessary for gardening prowess, but they are certainly a convenience, especially for the person who can't work outdoors too much or bend or stoop a great deal. Commercial greenhouses are available in many styles, and some of the smaller models can certainly add to and extend your gardening season. But you might want to try to design your own greenhouse, in which case you can plan accordingly and have raised benches to fit your stature, shelves not too high but within your reach, and many other arrangements developed just for you. It's a great way to garden year-round because greenhouses are excellent for starting seeds, propagating cuttings, growing flowers and house plants, and so forth.

A Typical Greenhouse

If you decide to get a greenhouse or have one built, study manufacturers' catalogs. See what ideas are good, and forget bad ones. Among the commercial greenhouses, the lean-to style, that is, the greenhouse that uses one wall of your house, is the most popular. There are many lean-to models: some need a concrete foundation, but others can be built on a concrete slab. Remember that the greenhouse adjacent to your home has the advantages of providing a pretty winter picture and of being easily accessible from your home. In Chicago, my mornings were always cheerful because the greenhouse adjoined the

A lean-to greenhouse gives the gardener a chance to garden all year; a definite plus. (Photo courtesy Lord & Burnham Inc.)

111

kitchen. I could enjoy morning coffee while viewing the flowers in their crystal palace as snow and sleet raged outdoors. Quite a comfortable feeling!

If it is impossible to put the greenhouse next to the house, consider a gallery leading from the house to the structure; this is like walking through a park arbor, and you never have to worry about inclement weather. Free-standing greenhouses are also available from suppliers. However, they are expensive and never made much sense to me.

A southern exposure is the best location for a greenhouse, but I have also seen lovely glass gardens on the east or west side of a home. Even in a north light you can grow lovely foliage plants, start seedlings, and so forth. In the south or southeast exposure the greenhouse benefits from winter sunlight; an eastern exposure is good because there is morning sun, and the unit that faces west will have bright light and some afternoon sun. Make your greenhouse large enough so you have space to work but not so large that it becomes a burden. A good size is 10 x 18 feet.

Your Own Greenhouse

Prefabricated commercial greenhouses come knocked down (unassembled), so putting them together is your job. Because this can be a complicated chore in spite of the many instruction sheets, planning and having your own unit built appeals to many people (and it really isn't that difficult) since you can have special things suited to your personal wants. The information you garner from greenhouse manufacturers' catalogs will tell you how the basic frame is made—follow this for your own design. Once you have the plan on paper, find a local carpenter who can do the job for you. Get prices and costs, and have him furnish all building materials and hardware. A carpenter is an ingenious man, and once he has a rough sketch of the greenhouse you want to have he can proceed to work with you on its final design.

Greenhouse Know-how

No matter what kind of gardening you decide to do in your greenhouse—sowing seeds, raising garden plants or house plants—there are certain plant conditions you'll have to maintain: the proper amount of humidity, correct temperatures, ventilation, and so forth.

Humidity: Try to maintain humidity at about 40 to 60 percent for such tropical plants as orchids, ferns, and bromeliads or for starting seeds. Humidity can be as low as 20 to 30 percent for cacti and succulents. The air will need more moisture as you increase the heat, and on very hot muggy days the humidity should also be high. At night, the humidity should be lower if you want good plant growth. Naturally, humidity will decrease at night.

Another fine greenhouse with brick foundation wall; note the roller blinds to protect plants from direct sun in summer. (Lord & Burnham Inc.)

Temperature: Most plants thrive with a daytime temperature of 60° to 75° F. and a 10- to 15-degree drop at night. However, avoid *sudden* temperature changes because they can harm plants. At about 6:00 start to gradually change the evening temperature. The minimum should be reached during the late night hours.

Ventilation: Because most plants need good air circulation (but with a minimum of drafts), open the ventilators during the day, even in very cold weather, to allow some air into the greenhouse. (Make sure the ventilators are opposite the side from which the wind is blowing.) In early spring the temperatures fluctuate unless you have thermostatic controls, so you may have to open and close vents

This greenhouse is equipped with automatic mist system, not really necessary for house plants. Benches are waist high and include cuttings of many plants. (USDA photo)

several times a day. Consider carefully the many different types of heating for the greenhouse: hot water, warm air, electric, and gas. You may have to call in a professional and let him recommend the best system for the greenhouse.

Watering: Too much shade and moisture can cause fungus disease on plants. Soil should be evenly moist for most plants, although resting ones need a somewhat drier soil. Mist plants early in the morning so the sun can dry them quickly.

Resting plants: This is a vital part of successful plant culture because most plants need a period of rest (lower temperatures and less water) at some time of the year. Generally, the resting time occurs after blooming. If your greenhouse is full of leaves instead of flowers, your plants aren't getting proper resting periods. Some part of the greenhouse will naturally have lower temperatures; this is the place to put resting plants.

Shading: Shading is generally applied in early spring and removed in fall. You can use shading paint or devise other means to protect plants from hot direct sun, which harms them. Roller blinds and trellises over the greenhouse that can easily be removed in winter (the bothersome chore of shading plants won't be necessary every year) are some of the other ways of shading plants.

Protection from insects: Keep a vigilant lookout for insects. When you see them, take immediate steps to eliminate them because once insects have a foothold they are difficult to eradicate. Use *botanical sprays only* when dealing with *insects;* poisonous chemicals are not necessary in the home greenhouse and should be avoided.